PAT BROWN, MBA

LacrosseMoney101

Using Lacrosse to Teach the Basics of Money

ABRAM · 47 · BROWN

First published by AbramBrown47 2026

First edition

ISBN: 978-1-967737-56-7

This book was professionally typeset on Reedsy.
Find out more at reedsy.com

Contents

Foreword

Lacrosse is a game of possession, patience, and vision.

Anyone who has played at a competitive level understands this quickly. You do not win by sprinting nonstop or firing shots the moment you touch the ball. You win by controlling space, valuing possession, moving the ball, trusting teammates, and making smart decisions over the course of a long game and a long season.

Money works the same way.

Yet for many athletes, especially lacrosse players, money enters their lives without a playbook. You spend years mastering footwork, stick skills, conditioning, and game IQ. You watch film. You learn systems. You accept coaching. But when it comes to money, most athletes are told to figure it out on their own, often right when the stakes are highest.

This book exists because that gap is real.

I've spent my life in locker rooms and meeting rooms. I played college football at a high level, where accountability was constant and structure was non-negotiable. After sports, I transitioned into financial services and built a career working with individuals, families, business owners, and athletes navigating increasingly complex financial lives. Over time, one pattern kept showing up.

Athletes are not bad with money.

They are undercoached.

They understand discipline.

They understand delayed gratification.

They understand preparation.

They understand long seasons.

What they are missing is translation.

Traditional financial education often feels disconnected from how athletes think and learn. It is abstract, jargon-heavy, and rarely tied to performance. Lacrosse players do not think in spreadsheets and formulas. They think in possessions, matchups, spacing, adjustments, and execution under pressure.

That is exactly how this book is written.

Lacrosse Money 101 uses the language, structure, and mindset of lacrosse to explain money in a way that makes sense to athletes. Not as theory. Not as fear-based warnings. But as a system you can learn, practice, and improve over time.

This is not a book about getting rich quickly.

It is not about hot tips or shortcuts.

It is not about perfection.

It is about controlling possession in your financial life.

Just like in lacrosse, most financial mistakes do not come from one catastrophic moment. They come from turnovers. Forcing plays. Ignoring fundamentals. Losing discipline when the game speeds up. Chasing shots instead of running the offense.

This book helps you slow the game down.

You will learn how to:

- Understand where your money actually goes
- Build systems that create consistency
- Protect yourself from unnecessary risk
- Invest with discipline instead of emotion
- Make adjustments as life changes
- Think long-term without losing urgency

Most importantly, you will learn how to treat money the way you treated your sport. With respect. With structure. With accountability.

Whether you are a current player, a recent graduate, or someone years removed from the game, the lessons still apply. Lacrosse teaches habits that translate far beyond the field. Vision. Communication. Trust. Awareness. Discipline under pressure.

Those habits can win financially too, if you apply them intentionally.

The long game matters.

In lacrosse, teams that value possession usually win. They may not always look flashy. They may not dominate highlights. But over four quarters, their discipline shows up on the scoreboard.

Money works the same way.

If you value possession, protect the ball, and make smart decisions consistently, the outcome takes care of itself.

This book is your playbook for doing exactly that.

Introduction

Every lacrosse player learns this lesson early, whether a coach says it directly or not.

You do not win by shooting the most.

You win by controlling possession.

Teams that panic, force shots, and try to score on every touch usually lose. Teams that value the ball, move it with purpose, read the field, and wait for the right opportunity tend to win over four quarters. Lacrosse is fast, physical, and chaotic, but the best teams always look calm. They play with vision. They understand when to attack and when to reset.

Money works the same way.

Most people think financial success comes from big moments. A big raise. A hot investment. A lucky break. A perfect purchase. Those moments are the financial equivalent of highlight-reel goals. They look impressive, but they are not what wins games consistently.

Winning financially is about possession.

It is about controlling your cash flow.

Protecting your resources.

Making disciplined decisions repeatedly.

Avoiding unnecessary turnovers.

Letting small advantages compound over time.

This book is built on that principle.

Why Athletes Struggle With Money Transitions

As an athlete, you grew up in a system that rewarded effort, discipline, and execution. Practices were scheduled. Expectations were clear. Feedback was immediate. You knew when you were improving because the results showed up on the field.

Money does not work that way.

There is no scoreboard that updates daily.

There is no coach calling timeouts.

There is no film session forcing you to review mistakes.

Financial consequences are delayed. A bad decision today may not hurt until years later. A good habit may feel unrewarding for a long time before it suddenly matters a lot. That delay is where most people lose possession.

Former athletes are especially vulnerable here. You are competitive. You are confident. You are used to pressure. But without structure, it is easy to force plays financially the same way inexperienced players force shots on the field.

This book helps you replace reaction with rhythm.

Possession Creates Options

In lacrosse, possession gives you options.

You can dodge.

You can pass.

You can reset.

You can change angles.

You can dictate tempo.

When you lose possession, your options disappear. You are suddenly reacting instead of controlling. The same thing happens financially.

When you live paycheck to paycheck, options shrink.

When debt piles up, decisions get forced.

When savings are thin, stress rises.

When money is unorganized, small problems become big ones.

Possession in money means having margin.
Cash reserves.
Low stress.
Flexibility.
Time to think before acting.
This book focuses on helping you build and protect that possession.

Discipline Beats Forcing Shots

Every lacrosse coach has yelled some version of the same message.
"Stop forcing it."
"Move the ball."
"Trust the offense."
"Value possession."
Those same messages apply to money.
Forcing shots financially looks like:

- Chasing hot investments
- Overspending to keep up
- Taking on debt without a plan
- Ignoring fundamentals because things feel fine
- Making emotional decisions under pressure

Discipline looks boring in the moment.
It also wins over time.
This book emphasizes systems, not willpower. Habits, not hype. Structure, not guesswork. Just like lacrosse, the goal is not perfection. The goal is consistency.

Playing the Long Game

Lacrosse seasons are long.

Careers are longer.

Life is longer still.

You do not win by dominating one quarter and disappearing in the fourth. You win by managing energy, making adjustments, and staying composed when the game gets tight.

Money is the same.

This book is not about shortcuts.

It is about building a game plan you can execute year after year.

It is about learning when to attack and when to reset.

It is about keeping possession so you can play on your terms.

If you approach money the way you approached lacrosse, with vision, discipline, and respect for fundamentals, you give yourself an advantage most people never develop.

You do not need to score on every possession.

You just need to keep the ball.

That is how games are won.

That is how financial success is built.

About This Book

Lacrosse is a thinking game.

From the outside, it looks fast and chaotic. Sticks flying. Bodies colliding. Shots coming from every angle. But anyone who has played at a competitive level knows the truth. Lacrosse rewards players who see the field, understand spacing, communicate, and stay disciplined when the game speeds up.

Money works the same way.

To people who have never studied it, money feels random. Markets move. Bills show up. Opportunities appear and disappear. Advice comes from everywhere. But underneath the noise is structure. Systems. Rules. Cause and effect. Once you understand how the game works, the chaos slows down.

This book exists to help you see money the way you learned to see lacrosse.

Why Lacrosse Is the Right Lens

Athletes learn best through experience, not theory. Lacrosse players, in particular, are trained to process information quickly, adapt under pressure, and execute within a system. You understand:

- Vision over tunnel focus
- Possession over panic
- Team offense over hero ball
- Defense and recovery over gambling
- Adjustments over excuses

Those same principles drive long-term financial success.

Traditional personal finance books often miss this connection. They explain money as a set of abstract rules instead of a living game that requires awareness, discipline, and execution. This book translates financial concepts into situations you already understand.

Not as metaphors for entertainment.

As frameworks for decision-making.

Money Is a Possession Game

At its core, money is about control.

Who controls their cash flow?

Who controls their risk?

Who controls their time?

Who controls their decisions under pressure?

Lacrosse teaches you early that possession creates leverage. When your team controls the ball, you dictate tempo. You force the defense to react. You create high-quality scoring opportunities instead of rushed attempts.

Financially, possession looks like:

- Having savings so you are not forced into bad decisions
- Managing debt so it does not control your options
- Investing consistently instead of chasing outcomes
- Making decisions calmly instead of emotionally

This book shows you how to build and protect that possession over time.

Discipline Over Flash

Lacrosse rewards discipline.

The best teams are not always the flashiest. They are the ones that clear cleanly, ride hard, communicate on slides, and execute when it matters. They win because they make fewer mistakes, not because they chase highlights.

Money works the same way.

Financial success rarely comes from one big play. It comes from hundreds of small, disciplined decisions:

- Spending intentionally
- Saving consistently
- Investing patiently
- Protecting against risk
- Adjusting when life changes

This book emphasizes fundamentals because fundamentals travel. They work whether you are earning a little or a lot, early in your career or late, in calm markets or volatile ones.

Built for Athletes, Not Economists

This book is written for current and former lacrosse players.

It assumes you understand:

- Practice and repetition
- Film study and adjustments
- Accountability and coaching
- Long seasons and delayed results
- Winning without always getting credit

It does not assume you have a background in finance.

There is no jargon for the sake of sounding smart. Concepts are explained clearly and tied directly to how you think as an athlete. The goal is not to turn you into a financial expert. The goal is to make you competent, confident, and disciplined enough to avoid mistakes and build momentum.

A Playbook, Not a Prediction

This is not a book about predicting markets.

It is not about timing the perfect moment.

It is not about guarantees.

It is a playbook.

Just like in lacrosse, you cannot control weather, referees, or opponents. You can control preparation, effort, discipline, and decision-making. This book focuses on what is in your control.

You will learn how to:

- Build a financial foundation
- Protect yourself from unnecessary risk
- Invest with patience instead of emotion
- Make smart adjustments as life evolves
- Stay composed when things get chaotic

Why This Matters After Lacrosse

When lacrosse ends, structure disappears.

No more mandatory practices.

No more coaches setting schedules.

No more teammates holding you accountable.

Money becomes one of the first places where that lack of structure shows up. This book helps you rebuild it.

It gives you a framework to approach money the way you approached the game. With intention. With discipline. With respect for the long season ahead.

You learned how to play lacrosse through reps, feedback, and coaching.

You can learn how to manage money the same way.

This book is here to help you do exactly that.

Foolish Assumptions

Every coach starts the season with assumptions.

Not about talent, but about mindset. About effort. About whether players will do the little things without being reminded. Those assumptions shape how a team practices, prepares, and competes.

This book does the same thing.

Before getting into tactics, systems, and strategy, it is important to be clear about what **Lacrosse Money 101** assumes about you. Not because everyone fits perfectly, but because these assumptions define how the material is presented and how it is meant to be used.

Some of these assumptions may feel uncomfortable. That is intentional.

Assumption One: You Are Capable of Discipline Without Supervision

This book assumes you can handle responsibility.

In lacrosse, discipline is enforced early. Miss practice and there are consequences. Skip film and you get exposed. Fail to communicate and the entire defense suffers. Accountability is immediate and obvious.

Money does not work that way.

There is no whistle when you overspend.

No coach pulls you aside when you delay saving.

No scoreboard flashes when small mistakes accumulate.

This book assumes you are willing to apply discipline even when no one is watching. Not perfectly, but consistently. If you are looking for motivation without responsibility, this is not that book.

Assumption Two: You Understand That Fundamentals Matter More Than Flash

Lacrosse players know this truth, even if they forget it sometimes.

Games are won by ground balls, clean clears, disciplined slides, and smart decisions. Highlights are fun. Fundamentals win.

This book assumes you are willing to focus on fundamentals in your financial life. Budgeting. Saving. Protecting against risk. Investing patiently. Adjusting when necessary.

If you are only interested in big plays, shortcuts, or quick wins, this book will feel slow. That is by design.

Assumption Three: You Are Willing to Look Honestly at Your Habits

Film does not lie.

Athletes improve because they review performance honestly. They accept correction. They identify weaknesses. They adjust.

Money requires the same honesty.

This book assumes you are willing to look at:

- How you actually spend
- Where your money goes
- How decisions are made under pressure
- Which habits help and which ones hurt

If you are not willing to examine behavior, no system will work. This book is not here to shame you. It is here to help you build awareness.

Assumption Four: You Respect the Long Game

Lacrosse seasons are long.

Careers are longer.

Life is longer still.

This book assumes you understand that meaningful results take time. That progress is rarely linear. That patience is a skill, not a personality trait.

If you expect immediate payoff from every decision, money will frustrate you. Just like forcing offense early in a game often leads to turnovers later.

This book is built for athletes who are willing to commit to steady progress over time.

Assumption Five: You Are Coachable

Being coachable does not mean being passive.

It means listening.

Testing ideas.

Applying feedback.

Making adjustments.

This book assumes you are open to learning, even if some concepts challenge what you have heard before. Locker room advice is not always correct. Family money myths are not always helpful. Cultural narratives about success are often misleading.

Lacrosse players learn to separate noise from instruction. This book expects the same.

Assumption Six: You Want Control, Not Just Outcomes

In lacrosse, control wins games.

Control of possession.

Control of spacing.

Control of tempo.

Control under pressure.

This book assumes you want control in your financial life. Not just more money, but less stress. Not just higher income, but more flexibility. Not just wins, but sustainability.

If your goal is only appearances, status, or comparison, the framework here will feel misaligned. This book is about control, clarity, and confidence over time.

Final Reality Check

These assumptions are not judgments.

They are expectations.

Just like a coach expects effort, communication, and accountability, this book expects engagement. You do not have to be perfect. You do have to participate.

If you bring the same mindset to money that you brought to lacrosse, discipline, patience, and respect for the system, you will be ahead of most people.

Not because you are smarter.

Because you are prepared to play the long game.

How This Playbook Is Organized

Lacrosse players learn best when there is a system.

You do not walk onto the field and improvise an offense. You learn fundamentals first. Then you layer in concepts. Then you adjust based on matchups, opponents, and situations. Everything builds on what came before.

This book is organized the same way.

Lacrosse Money 101 is not meant to be read like a novel or skimmed for quick answers. It is a playbook. Each section builds on the last, creating a complete system for managing money over the course of a long season and a long life.

Built Like a Lacrosse Season

The book follows the natural progression of an athlete's development and career.

You start with fundamentals.

You learn to protect possession.

You build an offense.

You make adjustments.

You prepare for the full season and life after the game.

Each part represents a phase where different skills matter more.

Skipping ahead without understanding the basics is like installing advanced sets before players can throw and catch consistently. You might get by for a while, but breakdowns show up under pressure.

Front Matter: Setting the Mindset

The opening sections establish how to think about money before getting into tactics.

This is where you learn:

- Why possession matters more than flashy plays
- How money mirrors the structure of lacrosse
- What assumptions this book makes about your discipline and mindset

This section sets expectations. It frames money as a system, not a guessing game. Without this foundation, everything else feels disconnected.

Part I: Stick Skills and Fundamentals

This is the base of the entire playbook.

Just like in lacrosse, if you cannot control the ball, nothing else works. This section focuses on awareness and control.

You will learn how to:

- Understand where your money actually goes
- Separate saving, investing, and gambling
- Build basic systems for budgeting and saving
- Avoid common early mistakes that cost possession

This section is not exciting. It is essential.

Teams that skip fundamentals turn the ball over. Financially, the same thing happens.

Part II: Defense, Slides, and Protection

Once you have possession, you have to protect it.

This section focuses on risk awareness and protection. Insurance, liability, and defensive decision-making are covered here. These topics rarely get attention until something goes wrong.

In lacrosse, great teams recover quickly. They slide early. They communicate. They protect the goal.

Financially, this section helps you:

- Understand different types of risk
- Protect income and assets
- Avoid mistakes that create long-term damage

Defense does not win highlights. It keeps you in the game.

Part III: Building the Offense

This is where investing fundamentals live.

Once you control possession and protect the ball, you can start building an offense. This section explains how markets work, how investments generate returns, and how to avoid forcing plays.

You will learn:

- What stocks, bonds, and funds actually are
- How risk and reward work together
- Why patience beats prediction
- How to invest without hero ball

This section emphasizes discipline, ball movement, and long-term execution over excitement.

Part IV: Managing the Game and Making Adjustments

Even the best game plan needs adjustments.

This section focuses on managing investments over time. Asset allocation, rebalancing, and decision-making under pressure live here.

In lacrosse, championships are won by teams that adjust without losing structure. Financially, the same is true.

This section helps you:

- Build balanced lineups
- Make changes without panic
- Adapt to life events without blowing up the system

Part V: The Full Season and Life After Lacrosse

Money decisions extend beyond investing.

This section covers taxes, housing, career decisions, retirement, and family conversations. These are the moments that shape long-term outcomes but often get rushed or avoided.

The focus here is sustainability.

Playing the full season.

Finishing strong.

Part VI: Winning the Long Game

The final section pulls everything together.

It addresses professional help, avoiding scams, and staying disciplined over decades. This is about maintaining structure when the spotlight is gone and habits matter most.

How to Use This Book

Read it in order.

Apply concepts gradually.

Revisit sections as life changes.

Just like lacrosse, mastery comes from repetition and adjustment, not one perfect read.

This playbook is designed to stay with you long after the final whistle.

About Pat Brown

Pat Brown's perspective on money, discipline, and long-term success was forged long before he entered the world of finance.

Pat played college football at the **University of Kansas from 1994 to 1999** and was named **team captain for the 1999 season**. His years in the locker room shaped how he views accountability, preparation, leadership, and responsibility. In that environment, excuses were exposed quickly, effort was non-negotiable, and performance mattered more than intentions. Those lessons did not disappear when football ended. They became the foundation for everything that followed.

After his playing career, Pat transitioned into financial services and built a career as a **financial advisor and wealth manager**, working with individuals, families, business owners, and athletes navigating increasingly complex financial lives. Over time, he saw a familiar pattern emerge. The people who struggled most were rarely lazy or unintelligent. They lacked structure, clarity, and a playbook that matched how they actually thought and learned.

Pat pursued advanced education and professional development to deepen his expertise, earning an **MBA** along with industry designations including **ChFC® (Chartered Financial Consultant®)**, **RICP® (Retirement Income Certified Professional®)**, and **CAP® (Chartered Advisor in Philanthropy®)**. His background blends academic training with real-world experience in financial planning, retirement income strategies, tax planning, risk management, and philanthropy.

As the college sports landscape shifted with the introduction of **Name, Image, and Likeness (NIL)** opportunities, Pat recognized a growing and urgent education gap. Student-athletes were suddenly gaining access to income, contracts, and endorsements without the financial knowledge needed to manage cash flow, taxes, business structures, and long-term consequences. Many were being handed opportunity before they were handed education.

That reality became the catalyst for Pat's work in the NIL space.

He has since become a recognized voice in athlete financial education and has been interviewed by national publications and platforms including **Financial Planning**, **Yahoo**, and **ESPN Andscape**, where he shares insights on NIL planning, financial literacy gaps, and the unique challenges facing student-athletes and their families.

These experiences led Pat to author a growing series of **practical, athlete-focused books** designed to meet athletes where they are, not where traditional financial education assumes they should be. His NIL-related titles include:

- *Financial Literacy for NIL*
- *Financial Literacy for NIL for Parents of Student Athletes*
- *Financial Literacy for NIL for High School Students*
- *Financial Literacy for NIL for International Student Athletes*

Each book is written to be clear, accessible, and grounded in real-world scenarios rather than theory or jargon.

Pat also created an expanding collection of **sport-specific financial education titles**, including *Football Money 101, Baseball Money 101, Basketball Money 101, Cheer Money 101, Dance Money 101, Gymnastics Money 101, Hockey Money 101, Lacrosse Money 101, Rowing Money 101, Soccer Money 101, Softball Money 101, Tennis Money 101, Track Money 101, Volleyball Money 101,* and *Wrestling Money 101.* Each book translates the culture, discipline, and mindset of a specific sport into financial lessons athletes can apply long after competition ends.

To extend this mission beyond books, Pat founded **Former Student Athlete**, a platform created to support athletes navigating life after sports. Former Student Athlete provides education, community, and real-world resources focused on financial literacy, career transitions, health, identity, and long-term success once the uniform comes off. More information can be found at:

- www.formerstudentathlete.com
- www.financialliteracyfornil.com
- www.financialliteracyforstudentathletes.com

Pat is easy to find through a Google search, on LinkedIn, or on Twitter, where he regularly shares insights on athletes, money, and life after sports. For questions specifically related to **Lacrosse Money 101**, he can be reached at:

info@lacrossemoney101.com

Pat's work is rooted in a belief shaped by both football and finance. **Athletes deserve a better playbook for life after sports, and financial education should arrive before opportunity turns into regret.**

Part I: Stick Skills and Fundamentals

You cannot score if you cannot control the ball.

Every lacrosse coach starts in the same place.

Before offenses.

Before rides.

Before man-up sets.

Before schemes and adjustments.

You start with stick skills.

Can you catch cleanly?

Can you throw accurately under pressure?

Can you protect the ball when contact comes?

Can you move it without panic?

If the answer is no, nothing else matters. You can have speed, strength, and talent, but without control, possession disappears and the game tilts quickly.

Money works exactly the same way.

Before investing.

Before building wealth.

Before chasing opportunity.

Before thinking long term.

You need control.

This first section of **Lacrosse Money 101** is about building that control. Not through complicated strategies or advanced concepts, but through fundamentals. The same way lacrosse fundamentals feel repetitive, boring, and unglamorous, until you realize they are the reason you stay on the field.

Why Fundamentals Come First

In lacrosse, fundamentals are not optional. You cannot skip wall ball and expect to handle pressure in a game. You cannot ignore ground balls and still expect to win possession battles. The basics show up whether you respect them or not.

Financial fundamentals work the same way.

If you do not know:

- Where your money comes from
- Where it goes
- What you owe
- What you own
- How cash flow actually works

Then every financial decision becomes harder than it needs to be. Opportunities feel stressful instead of exciting. Mistakes feel bigger. Progress feels inconsistent.

This section is designed to remove confusion by creating clarity.

Control Creates Confidence

Lacrosse players play faster when they trust their stick.

When you know you can catch in traffic, you do not rush. When you trust your fundamentals, the game slows down. You see the field better. You make smarter decisions. You stop forcing plays.

Money behaves the same way.

When your finances are organized, you stop reacting emotionally. You do not panic when something unexpected happens. You do not feel pressure to chase quick fixes. You make decisions calmly because you understand your position.

Control creates confidence.

Confidence creates patience.

Patience creates better outcomes.

The Cost of Skipping This Section

Many people want to jump straight to investing.

That is like installing advanced offensive sets before players can throw and catch. It might work in practice. It breaks down in games.

If you skip budgeting, saving, and awareness, investing becomes stressful instead of strategic. Debt feels heavier. Risk feels scarier. Every decision feels urgent.

This section prevents that.

It teaches you how to:

- Track income and expenses honestly
- Build systems instead of relying on willpower
- Separate needs from wants
- Avoid common mistakes that lead to financial turnovers
- Protect possession before trying to score

None of this is exciting.

All of it is necessary.

Discipline Over Talent

Lacrosse rewards disciplined teams.

The most talented roster does not always win. Teams that value possession, execute cleanly, and avoid unnecessary turnovers usually come out ahead over a full game and a full season.

Financially, the same truth applies.

You do not need to be a financial expert.

You do not need perfect timing.

You do not need special opportunities.

You need discipline.

You need awareness.

You need consistency.

This section assumes you are willing to do the unglamorous work. The daily reps. The boring checks. The habits that do not show immediate payoff but compound quietly.

Setting the Tone for the Rest of the Book

Everything that comes later builds on this foundation.

Defense only works if you protect possession.

Offense only works if you control tempo.

Adjustments only matter if you know your baseline.

Part I sets that baseline.

It teaches you how to handle the ball in your financial life so that when pressure comes, and it will, you are prepared. Not because you are guessing, but because you have trained for it.

You cannot score if you cannot control the ball.

This section teaches you how to do exactly that.

Chapter 1: Why Money Feels Confusing After Lacrosse

The first time the confusion hits usually is not dramatic.

You are done with practice.

The season is over.

Your schedule opens up.

Money starts moving differently.

Maybe it is your first real paycheck. Maybe it is NIL income. Maybe it is a summer job, a bonus, or a contract. There is no coach pulling you aside to explain what to do next. No film session. No whiteboard. Just decisions you are expected to make correctly, without training.

For lacrosse players, this moment feels unfamiliar because money is a game you were never coached to play.

Why Financial Literacy Is Rarely Taught to Athletes

From the time you picked up a stick, your environment was built around performance.

Coaches taught you how to dodge, pass, shoot, defend, ride, and recover. Strength coaches handled the weight room. Trainers handled your body. Academic advisors handled eligibility. Schedules were set. Expectations were clear.

Money never made the cut.

Not because it does not matter, but because it was assumed to be someone else's job. Parents. Schools. Advisors. Future you.

Lacrosse culture reinforces this. You are taught to focus on the next rep, the next drill, the next game. Long-term thinking exists, but it is almost always framed around athletic development, not financial outcomes.

So when the uniform comes off, or when income starts flowing before you are ready, you are handed responsibility without preparation. That is not a personal failure. It is a structural gap.

Money Myths Passed Through Locker Rooms and Sidelines

When education is missing, myths fill the space.

You have probably heard some version of these:

"I'll deal with money later."

"Once I make more, this will be easy."

"Investing is just picking the right stock."

"Debt is normal."

"Everyone is broke in their 20s."

"I'll figure it out after the season."

These ideas spread the same way bad habits spread in practice. One teammate says it. Another repeats it. Eventually it feels true because it is familiar.

In lacrosse terms, this is like believing you can skip wall ball and still have great hands. It might work for a while. Eventually, pressure exposes the weakness.

Money myths feel harmless early. They become expensive later.

Saving vs Investing vs Gambling

One of the biggest sources of confusion is that saving, investing, and gambling often get lumped together.

They are not the same.

Saving is possession.

It is control.

It is money set aside for stability, emergencies, and near-term needs.

In lacrosse terms, saving is cradling through pressure instead of forcing a pass. It is boring. It keeps the ball safe.

Investing is structured offense.

It is a long-term plan designed to create growth over time. It involves risk, but that risk is intentional and managed.

In lacrosse terms, investing is running a settled offense. Ball movement. Patience. High-percentage looks.

Gambling is forcing shots.

It is chasing quick wins without a plan. It relies on luck more than discipline.

In lacrosse terms, gambling is shooting from bad angles, early in the shot clock, hoping something good happens.

The problem is that all three can look similar on the surface. Money moves. Accounts change. Someone wins big and talks about it. The difference is not the outcome in one moment. The difference is the process.

Athletes who struggle financially often confuse gambling with investing and call it confidence.

Why Discipline Beats Forcing Shots

Lacrosse punishes forcing plays.

You might score once.

You might even score twice.

But turnovers add up.

Financially, forcing shots looks like:

- Chasing hot investments
- Overspending after a win
- Ignoring fundamentals because things feel good
- Making decisions based on emotion instead of structure

Discipline, on the other hand, looks slow.

It looks like budgeting.

It looks like saving consistently.

It looks like investing the same way when markets are boring.

It looks like saying no when you could say yes.

In lacrosse, disciplined teams control tempo. They protect possession. They trust the system. Over time, they win more often than teams built on chaos.

Money works the same way.

Why Athletes Feel Behind Even When They Are Not

Many former lacrosse players feel late to the game financially.

You look around and assume everyone else knows something you do not. Social media reinforces that feeling. Highlight reels are everywhere. Mistakes are hidden.

The truth is simpler.

Most people are guessing.

Most people never learned this either.

Most people are reacting instead of planning.

The difference is that athletes are used to clear feedback. Scoreboards. Stats. Film. Money provides delayed feedback. Mistakes do not show up immediately. Wins are quiet. Losses compound silently.

That delay makes confusion feel personal, even when it is structural.

Coach's Perspective

A lacrosse coach would not sugarcoat this.

"Control the ball."

"Stop forcing it."

"Do the boring work."

"Trust the system."

"Possession wins games."

Financial discipline is the same conversation in a different language.

You do not need to be perfect.

You need to stop turning the ball over.

You need to build habits you can repeat under pressure.

Game Situations and Decision Points

You get paid more than you ever have before.

Do you protect possession or force a shot?

You hear about an investment that made someone rich.

Do you chase it or stick to your plan?

You feel behind because others look ahead.

Do you rush or slow the game down?

Every decision is a possession.

Common Athlete Mistakes and Financial Parallels

Lacrosse players force shots under pressure.

Financially, that becomes chasing quick money.

Lacrosse players skip fundamentals when bored.

Financially, that becomes ignoring budgeting and saving.

Lacrosse players confuse confidence with recklessness.

Financially, that becomes gambling dressed up as investing.

Winning the Long Game

Money feels confusing after lacrosse because the structure disappeared, not because you are incapable.

This book exists to rebuild that structure.

You do not win lacrosse by scoring once.

You win by controlling possession for four quarters.

Money is no different.

Discipline beats forcing shots.

Every time.

Athlete Takeaways

- Protect possession before trying to score
- Discipline wins more games than talent alone
- Saving, investing, and gambling are not the same play
- Forcing shots creates turnovers in money and lacrosse
- Slow the game down and trust the system

Chapter 2: See the Whole Field

Your Financial Snapshot

The best lacrosse players do not stare at the ball.

They see the whole field.

They know where the slide is coming from. They sense pressure before it arrives. They understand spacing, timing, and matchups without needing to be told. That vision is not accidental. It comes from film, reps, and awareness.

Money works the same way.

Most financial mistakes are not caused by bad intentions. They happen because people are playing with tunnel vision. They react to what is directly in front of them without understanding how everything else connects.

A financial snapshot is how you lift your head, scan the field, and understand the game you are actually playing.

Opening Story From the Sport

Think about a fast break.

You pick up the ball in transition. You have options. You can dodge, pass, or shoot. The decision happens fast, but it is not random. You already know where your teammates are, who is trailing, and where the defense is vulnerable.

Now imagine trying to make that decision without seeing the field. No awareness of spacing. No idea who is open. You might still make a play, but it is more likely to end in a turnover.

That is how most people operate financially. They make decisions without seeing the whole picture.

Income, Expenses, and Cash Flow

Financially, income is your possession source.

It is where the ball comes from.

Salary. Wages. NIL income. Bonuses. Side work. Scholarships. Support from family. All of it counts.

Expenses are how possession gets used.

Rent. Food. Transportation. Training. Entertainment. Travel. Subscriptions. These are your passes, dodges, and shots.

Cash flow is what happens when you compare the two.

If more money comes in than goes out, you have positive cash flow. If more goes out than comes in, you are playing defense the entire game.

In lacrosse terms, cash flow is game tempo. If you are constantly chasing, recovering, and scrambling, fatigue sets in. When you control tempo, the game slows down and options open up.

Many athletes struggle here because income feels unpredictable early. That makes it tempting to ignore structure. But even uneven income needs awareness. You cannot manage what you do not track.

Assets, Liabilities, and Net Worth

Assets are what you own that have value.

Cash.

Savings.

Investments.

Retirement accounts.

Vehicles.

Property.

Liabilities are what you owe.

Credit cards.

Student loans.

Car loans.

Personal loans.

Net worth is the difference between the two.

Assets minus liabilities.

In lacrosse terms, net worth is not one highlight. It is the scoreboard after four quarters. You can score early and still lose if turnovers pile up. You can start slow and win if execution improves.

Athletes often focus on income and ignore net worth. That is like focusing on shots taken instead of goals scored. What matters is the outcome, not just activity.

Tracking net worth does not require perfection. It requires honesty. It shows whether you are building ground or giving it back.

Fixed vs Variable Expenses

Not all expenses behave the same way.

Fixed expenses are predictable.

Rent.

Insurance.

Loan payments.

Subscriptions.

Variable expenses change.

Food.

Entertainment.

Travel.

Gear.

Lifestyle spending.

In lacrosse terms, fixed expenses are your base defense. They are always on the field. Variable expenses are your matchups and adjustments.

You cannot eliminate all fixed expenses, but you can choose how many you commit to. Too many fixed obligations reduce flexibility. That matters early in a career.

Variable expenses are where discipline shows up. This is where most athletes either gain control or lose it. Small, repeated choices compound quickly.

The mistake is assuming variable means unimportant. In reality, variable expenses determine whether you can save, invest, or breathe.

Reviewing Where Your Money Actually Goes

This is the hardest part.

Not because it is complicated, but because it removes denial.

Most people believe they know where their money goes. Very few have actually looked.

Reviewing spending is film study.

You do not watch film to beat yourself up. You watch to understand patterns. Where did possessions break down? Where did spacing fail? Where did effort slip?

Financially, this means pulling bank statements and credit card activity and categorizing spending. Not once. Regularly.

Patterns will appear.

Subscriptions you forgot about.

Impulse spending.

Expenses that do not align with priorities.

Areas where money leaks quietly.

This is not about shame. It is about clarity. Teams that refuse to watch film do not improve. People who refuse to review spending stay stuck.

Why Athletes Avoid the Snapshot

Athletes avoid this step for familiar reasons.

It feels boring.

It feels uncomfortable.

It feels like judgment.

In sports, you cannot avoid the scoreboard. In money, you can ignore it for a long time. That delay creates false confidence.

Seeing the whole field requires maturity. It means accepting where you are without panic or ego.

Once you see clearly, decisions become easier.

Coach's Perspective

A lacrosse coach would be direct.

"Know the situation."

"Lift your head."

"See the whole field."

"You cannot fix what you refuse to see."

"Awareness comes before execution."

This chapter is not about changing anything yet. It is about understanding the game you are currently in.

Game Situations and Decision Points

You feel stressed about money.

Do you guess, or do you review?

You want to save more.

Do you assume it is impossible, or do you look for leaks?

You feel behind others.

Do you compare highlights, or do you check your own scoreboard?

Vision determines decisions.

Common Athlete Mistakes and Financial Parallels

Lacrosse players play with tunnel vision.

Financially, that leads to reactionary decisions.

Lacrosse players avoid film after losses.

Financially, that leads to repeated mistakes.

Lacrosse players focus on effort instead of execution.

Financially, that leads to busy activity without progress.

Winning the Long Game

You cannot control possession if you cannot see the field.

A financial snapshot is not about judgment. It is about control. Once you understand income, expenses, assets, and liabilities, the game slows down.

From here, rhythm becomes possible.

Athlete Takeaways

- Lift your head and see the whole field
- Cash flow controls tempo
- Net worth is the real scoreboard
- Fixed expenses limit flexibility
- Film study creates clarity before change

Chapter 3: Controlling Possession

Budgeting and Saving

In lacrosse, possession wins games.

You can have the best shooters on the field, the fastest dodgers, and the most creative offense, but if you cannot hold the ball, none of it matters. Ground balls, clean catches, smart passes, and patience are what give you chances to score.

Money works the same way.

You do not build wealth by taking wild shots. You build it by controlling possession. Budgeting and saving are not about restriction. They are about control, rhythm, and giving yourself repeated opportunities to advance the ball.

Opening Story From the Sport

Think about a long offensive possession late in the game.

You are up one goal. The defense is tired. The crowd wants a shot. But instead of forcing something, your team settles in. You swing the ball. You protect it. You make the defense move. Eventually, a high-percentage opportunity opens up.

That possession does not happen by accident. It happens because everyone understands their role and values the ball.

Budgeting and saving work the same way. They slow the game down and put you in control.

Budgeting Systems That Actually Work

Most athletes hate the word budget.

It sounds like limitation. Like being told no. Like losing freedom.

That is a misunderstanding.

A budget is not a restriction. It is a game plan.

Financially, a budget is simply deciding where money goes before it disappears. It answers three questions.

How much comes in?

Where does it need to go?

What gets priority?

In lacrosse terms, budgeting is offensive structure. You still play fast. You still attack. But you do it with purpose.

The best budgeting systems are simple.

Track income.

Identify fixed expenses.

Set intentional limits for variable spending.

Decide what gets saved first.

If the system is too complicated, it will not last. Complexity leads to hesitation. Hesitation leads to turnovers.

The goal is consistency, not perfection.

Automating Savings Like Consistent Reps

In lacrosse, you do not rely on motivation to practice fundamentals.

You do reps.

Ground balls. Passing drills. Shooting form. Over and over again. The work happens whether you feel like it or not.

Saving money works the same way.

Automation is the financial equivalent of reps.

Automatic transfers to savings.

Automatic retirement contributions.

Automatic investment funding.

When saving is automatic, it stops being a decision. It becomes part of the system. That removes emotion, excuses, and fatigue.

Athletes who try to save only when they feel motivated struggle. Just like players who only train when inspired never reach consistency.

Reps matter in sports. They matter with money too.

Emergency Funds as Injury Protection

Every athlete understands injury risk.

You train to reduce it. You warm up. You tape ankles. You have trainers. You do not assume injuries will happen, but you prepare because they might.

An emergency fund serves the same role financially.

It protects you from unexpected hits.

Car repairs.

Medical bills.

Job changes.

Travel emergencies.

Family needs.

Without an emergency fund, every unexpected expense becomes a crisis. With one, problems stay contained.

In lacrosse terms, an emergency fund is your slide package. When something breaks down, help is already moving.

A basic emergency fund is usually three to six months of essential expenses. Not lifestyle. Not luxury. Survival.

This is not exciting money. It does not score goals. But it prevents losses that derail entire seasons.

Balancing Lifestyle With Long-Term Goals

This is where many athletes struggle.

You work hard.

You sacrifice.

You finally earn money.

You want to enjoy it.

That desire is normal.

The mistake is thinking enjoyment and discipline are opposites.

They are not.

In lacrosse terms, this is understanding shot selection. You can take shots. You just do not take bad ones repeatedly.

Financially, balance means enjoying money intentionally while still protecting the future.

That might look like:

Choosing experiences over constant upgrades.

Spending freely in a few areas that matter and limiting others.

Increasing savings as income grows instead of increasing lifestyle at the same pace.

Lifestyle creep is the silent opponent. It does not announce itself. It just slowly eats possession.

Athletes who plan enjoyment keep control. Athletes who spend reactively lose it.

Why Discipline Beats Forcing Shots

Forcing shots feels productive.

So does forcing spending.

New gear.

New car.

New place.

New status symbols.

None of those guarantee progress.

In lacrosse, forcing shots leads to turnovers and fast breaks the other way. In money, forcing spending leads to stress, debt, and lost flexibility.

Discipline feels boring. It looks quiet. It does not get attention.

But discipline keeps possession.

The athletes who win long seasons understand this difference. They do not chase highlights. They value control.

Coach's Perspective

A coach would not overcomplicate it.

"Value the ball."

"Protect possession."

"Do not force it."

"Reps matter."

"Control the tempo."

Budgeting and saving are not about being conservative. They are about being smart.

Game Situations and Decision Points

You get paid.

Do you save first or spend first?

An unexpected expense hits.

Do you panic or use protection?

Your income increases.

Do you increase savings or lifestyle immediately?

Every decision either protects possession or gives it away.

Common Athlete Mistakes and Financial Parallels

Lacrosse players force shots under pressure.

Financially, that leads to impulse spending.

Lacrosse players skip fundamentals.

Financially, that leads to inconsistent saving.

Lacrosse players rely on talent alone.

Financially, that leads to poor systems.

Winning the Long Game

Possession is not flashy, but it wins.

Budgeting gives you awareness. Saving gives you protection. Automation gives you consistency. Balance gives you sustainability.

You do not need perfect execution. You need steady control.

That is how championships are built. That is how wealth is built.

Athlete Takeaways

- Possession matters more than highlights
- A budget is a game plan, not a restriction
- Automation turns saving into reps
- Emergency funds protect you from hard hits
- Discipline keeps control when pressure rises

Chapter 4: Credit, Debt, and Turnovers

How Credit Can Help or Hurt Your Game

In lacrosse, turnovers change everything.

You can dominate possession for minutes, execute clean passes, and control tempo, but one careless turnover flips the field instantly. Now you are playing defense. Momentum shifts. Pressure increases. One mistake can erase a lot of good work.

Credit and debt work the same way.

Used well, credit helps you advance the ball. Used poorly, it creates turnovers that cost you possession, flexibility, and long-term control. This chapter is not about avoiding credit entirely. It is about understanding how it works, when it helps, and when it quietly hurts you.

Opening Story From the Sport

Think about a rushed clear under pressure.

The defense slides hard. You feel the clock. Instead of making the simple pass, you try to force a risky outlet upfield. The ball gets picked off. Now your team is scrambling, and you are defending a fast break.

The mistake was not effort. It was decision-making.

Credit mistakes usually look the same. They happen when urgency replaces discipline.

How Credit Scores and Reports Actually Work

A credit score is not a judgment of character. It is a tool lenders use to measure risk.

At its core, your credit score answers one question: how likely are you to repay what you borrow?

Credit reports track:

- Payment history
- Amounts owed
- Length of credit history
- Types of credit used
- New credit activity

In lacrosse terms, your credit score is like your reputation as a ball carrier. Coaches and teammates trust players who protect the ball. Lenders trust borrowers who pay consistently and do not overextend.

The biggest factor is payment history. Late payments are turnovers. Even one can hurt more than people expect.

Credit scores improve slowly and drop quickly. Just like possession, they are easier to protect than to recover.

Credit Cards, Loans, and Interest

Credit cards are tools. Not income. Not free money.

When used correctly, credit cards help build credit history, provide convenience, and sometimes offer rewards. When used incorrectly, they become high-interest traps.

Interest is the cost of borrowing money. It is how lenders get paid. Credit card interest rates are usually high because the debt is unsecured.

In lacrosse terms, interest is like defensive pressure. The longer you hold the ball in a bad position, the harder it becomes to get out cleanly.

Loans work similarly but with more structure.

Student loans.

Auto loans.

Personal loans.

Mortgages.

Each comes with different rates, terms, and consequences. The key difference is whether the loan helps you build long-term value or simply supports consumption.

Good Debt vs Bad Debt

Not all debt is equal.

Good debt is typically associated with long-term benefit or opportunity.

Examples might include:

- Education that increases earning power
- A reasonably priced home aligned with income
- Business investments with a clear plan

Bad debt usually funds short-term wants with long-term costs.

Examples include:

- High-interest credit card balances
- Financing depreciating items at long terms
- Lifestyle spending you cannot afford

In lacrosse terms, good debt is a smart dodge that creates space. Bad debt is forcing a shot into a double team.

The difference is intention, structure, and payoff.

Debt should support progress, not replace discipline.

How Debt Quietly Costs Possession

Debt rarely feels dangerous at first.

Payments seem manageable.

Balances feel abstract.

Minimum payments look small.

Over time, debt reduces flexibility.

It limits saving.

It increases stress.

It forces future decisions.

It narrows options.

In lacrosse terms, debt is playing with a shorter bench. You can still compete, but every mistake costs more because you have less margin.

The more debt you carry, the more your money works for someone else instead of for you.

Common Debt Traps Athletes Fall Into

Athletes are especially vulnerable to certain traps.

Easy approval.

Irregular income.

Peer pressure.

Reward mentality.

Lack of education.

Credit card companies know this.

Many athletes get approved for cards before they understand interest. Others use debt to smooth inconsistent income without a plan to repay it.

The most dangerous habit is normalizing debt. When carrying balances feels normal, turnovers become routine.

Using Credit Without Losing Control

Credit does not have to be avoided. It has to be managed.

Pay balances in full when possible.

Keep utilization low.

Make payments on time, every time.

Avoid stacking multiple obligations at once.

In lacrosse terms, this is ball protection. Two hands. Head up. Simple passes.

You do not need to be aggressive with credit. You need to be disciplined.

Coach's Perspective

A coach would keep it blunt.

"Value the ball."

"Do not force it."

"Make the simple play."

"Protect possession."

"Smart decisions win games."

Credit is not about flash. It is about control.

Game Situations and Decision Points

You are offered easy credit.

Do you ask how it fits your plan or just take it?

You carry a balance.

Do you attack it intentionally or let it linger?

Your income changes.

Do you adjust spending or keep borrowing?

Every decision either protects possession or gives it away.

Common Athlete Mistakes and Financial Parallels

Lacrosse players force passes under pressure.

Financially, that leads to impulse borrowing.

Lacrosse players ignore fundamentals.

Financially, that leads to missed payments.

Lacrosse players chase highlights.

Financially, that leads to lifestyle debt.

Winning the Long Game

Credit is not the enemy. Turnovers are.

When you understand how credit works, you can use it strategically. When you ignore it, it quietly controls you.

Protect possession.

Avoid forcing plays.

Stay disciplined.

That is how you keep momentum on your side for the long season.

Athlete Takeaways

- Credit is a tool, not free money
- Turnovers happen when urgency replaces discipline
- Interest is pressure that grows over time
- Good debt supports progress, bad debt costs possession
- Protect the ball and protect your future

Chapter 5: The Equipment Bag of Money: Banking Basics

Knowing What You Carry and How to Use It

Every lacrosse player knows their equipment bag matters.

You do not just throw sticks, pads, gloves, and cleats into a pile and hope it works out. Everything has a place. Each piece serves a specific purpose. If something is missing or misused, it shows up fast when the game speeds up.

Your banking system is your equipment bag for money.

Checking accounts, savings accounts, transfers, and protections are not exciting, but they determine how smoothly everything else works. When banking is sloppy, financial mistakes multiply. When it is organized, money flows cleanly and supports every other decision.

Opening Story From the Sport

Think about showing up to a game and realizing your equipment is wrong.

Wrong stick.

Missing mouthguard.

Cleats left at home.

Gloves soaked and unusable.

You might still play, but nothing feels right. Every rep is harder than it needs to be. Small distractions pull your focus away from execution.

Poor banking does the same thing financially. It creates friction, stress, and mistakes before you even get to investing or long-term planning.

Checking vs Savings Accounts: Different Tools, Different Jobs

Checking and savings accounts are not interchangeable.

A checking account is for movement.

Paychecks land here.

Bills get paid from here.

Daily spending flows through here.

A savings account is for holding.

Emergency funds.

Short-term goals.

Money you do not want to touch casually.

In lacrosse terms, your checking account is your stick in play. It moves constantly. Your savings account is your backup gear on the sideline. You do not use it every possession, but when you need it, it must be ready.

Problems happen when roles blur.

If all your money sits in checking, spending becomes too easy. If savings is hard to access or unclear, emergencies turn into debt.

Clean separation creates discipline without willpower.

Online Banks vs Traditional Banks

Not all banks operate the same way.

Traditional banks offer physical branches, in-person service, and familiarity. Online banks often offer higher interest on savings, lower fees, and strong digital tools.

Neither is automatically better.

In lacrosse terms, this is choosing equipment brands. Some players prefer familiarity and feel. Others prioritize performance and efficiency. What matters is fit and execution.

Key factors to evaluate:

- Fees and minimum balances
- Interest rates on savings
- Mobile app quality
- Customer service access
- Ease of transfers

The goal is not loyalty. The goal is functionality.

If your bank creates friction, confusion, or unnecessary cost, it is slowing you down.

How Money Moves Electronically

Money moves more often than people realize.

Direct deposit.

Automatic bill pay.

Transfers between accounts.

Peer-to-peer payments.

Debit and credit card transactions.

Understanding these systems prevents mistakes.

Automatic systems are powerful. They create consistency. But they also require monitoring. A missed transfer or incorrect setup can cause overdrafts or missed payments.

In lacrosse terms, this is ball movement. Clean passes keep the offense flowing. Lazy passes get picked off.

You need to know:

- When money comes in
- When money goes out
- Which accounts are connected
- What is automated and what is manual

Clarity beats complexity.

Overdrafts: Small Mistakes With Real Consequences

Overdrafts are one of the most common and avoidable banking errors.

An overdraft happens when you spend more than what is available in your checking account. Banks often charge fees for this. Those fees add up quietly.

In lacrosse terms, overdrafts are stepping out of bounds under no pressure. The mistake is unnecessary and costly.

Ways to reduce overdraft risk:

- Keep a buffer in checking
- Link savings for overdraft protection
- Set alerts for low balances
- Review transactions regularly

Overdraft fees are pure friction. They provide no benefit and drain momentum.

Fraud and Protecting Yourself

Fraud is part of modern finance.

Stolen card numbers.

Phishing emails.

Fake payment requests.

Unauthorized transactions.

This is not about paranoia. It is about awareness.

In lacrosse terms, this is defensive communication. You call out cutters. You slide early. You protect the middle.

Basic protections include:

- Strong, unique passwords

- Two-factor authentication
- Monitoring transactions
- Avoiding public Wi-Fi for banking
- Acting quickly if something looks wrong

Banks have protections, but speed matters. The faster you act, the easier it is to fix problems.

Ignoring fraud does not make it go away.

Why Banking Fundamentals Matter More Than People Think

Many athletes want to skip banking and jump straight to investing.

That is a mistake.

If cash flow is unclear, investing becomes stressful. If accounts are disorganized, saving feels inconsistent. If overdrafts and fees are constant, progress stalls.

In lacrosse terms, this is trying to run advanced plays without stick skills. You might get lucky sometimes, but consistency will be impossible.

Banking is the base layer. Everything else builds on it.

Coach's Perspective

A coach would keep it simple.

"Have your gear ready."

"Know your responsibilities."

"Do not beat yourself with mistakes."

"Handle the basics first."

"Details matter."

Banking basics are details. Details win games.

Game Situations and Decision Points

You open a new account.

Do you understand fees and rules or just sign up?

You automate payments.

Do you monitor them or assume they work forever?

You see a small fee.

Do you ignore it or fix the system?

Every small decision either cleans up your game or adds friction.

Common Athlete Mistakes and Financial Parallels

Players show up unprepared.

Financially, that looks like disorganized accounts.

Players ignore fundamentals.

Financially, that looks like overdrafts and fees.

Players assume equipment will work itself out.

Financially, that looks like unmanaged automation.

Winning the Long Game

Banking is not about maximizing returns. It is about minimizing mistakes.

When your equipment bag is organized, the game slows down. Decisions get easier. Stress drops. Execution improves.

Clean systems create confidence.

Handle your banking like you handle your gear. With intention, discipline, and respect for the basics.

Athlete Takeaways

- Checking and savings accounts have different jobs
- Clean separation creates discipline without effort
- Fees and overdrafts are preventable turnovers

- Automation works best when monitored
- Strong banking fundamentals support every other financial move

Part II: Defense, Slides, and Protection

Great Teams Recover Quickly and Protect the Goal

No matter how strong your offense is, lacrosse games are often decided on the defensive end.

Fast breaks happen. Turnovers occur. Someone gets beat topside. What separates good teams from great ones is not whether mistakes happen, but how quickly the defense slides, communicates, and recovers. A single breakdown does not have to become a goal if the system holds.

Your financial life works the same way.

Unexpected events will happen. Injuries. Car accidents. Job changes. Market swings. Bills you did not plan for. You cannot prevent every risk, but you can build protection so one mistake or one bad break does not flip the game.

This section is about defense. Not fear-based defense, but smart, disciplined protection that allows you to keep playing aggressively on offense.

Defense Is About Structure, Not Panic

In lacrosse, good defense is not just individual talent. It is communication. Positioning. Knowing when to slide and when to stay home. Everyone has a role, and everyone trusts the system.

Financial protection works the same way.

Insurance, emergency savings, and risk awareness are not exciting. They do not show up on highlight reels. But when something goes wrong, they are the difference between a minor disruption and a season-ending collapse.

Protection is not about expecting the worst.

It is about being prepared so you can recover quickly.

Slides Are Built Before the Game Starts

Defensive slides do not happen by accident.

They are drilled in practice. Everyone knows where help is coming from. Everyone knows who covers next. When the ball moves fast, the defense reacts automatically.

Financial slides are the same.

Emergency funds.

Insurance coverage.

Clear beneficiaries.

Cash reserves.

Proper account structure.

These are built before something goes wrong. When life speeds up, you do not want to be making decisions from scratch. You want systems that activate automatically.

If you wait to think about protection until after a problem hits, you are already late.

Risk Is Not the Enemy, Unmanaged Risk Is

Lacrosse is a contact sport. Risk is part of the game.

You dodge.

You cut.

You take hits.

You play through traffic.

But you do not play recklessly. You wear pads. You communicate. You trust your teammates to slide when needed.

Financially, risk is unavoidable too.

You cannot eliminate uncertainty. You can manage it. Understanding risk helps you decide when to push and when to reset. When to take chances and when to protect position.

The goal is not zero risk.

The goal is survivable risk.

Protection Allows You to Play Faster

The best defenses allow teams to play confidently.

When you trust the slide, you can pressure the ball harder. When you trust your goalie, you can extend out. When you trust the system, you play aggressive without panic.

Financial protection creates the same freedom.

When you have an emergency fund, unexpected expenses do not derail everything else. When you have proper insurance, one accident does not wipe out years of progress. When your basics are covered, you can invest, plan, and grow without constant fear.

Defense supports offense.

One Breakdown Does Not Have to Be a Goal

Every defense gets beaten sometimes.

What matters is recovery.

Missed slide.

Late communication.

Bad angle.

Great teams recover and limit damage. Poor teams freeze, blame, and compound the mistake.

Financially, setbacks happen too.

Unexpected bills.

Market drops.

Career detours.

The difference is not avoiding every problem. It is having enough protection that problems do not turn into permanent losses.

Defense keeps you alive in the game.

Coach's Perspective

A coach would be clear.

"Talk on defense."

"Slide early."

"Protect the middle."

"Do your job."

"Next play."

Protection is about responsibility. Everyone has a role, and when one player freelances, the whole unit suffers.

Why This Section Matters Before Investing

Many athletes want to skip defense and jump straight to offense.

Investing.

Side income.

Big purchases.

But without protection, growth is fragile.

One injury.

One lawsuit.

One uncovered loss.

This section builds the foundation that allows everything else to work. Just like defense sets the tone for the entire game, financial protection sets the tone for long-term success.

Great teams recover quickly.

Great financial plans do too.

You cannot win if every mistake ends in a goal.

Defense keeps you in the game long enough to win the season.

Chapter 6: Risk Awareness and Smart Decision Making

In lacrosse, risk is everywhere.

Every dodge carries risk. Every pass through traffic carries risk. Every slide creates exposure somewhere else on the field. You cannot play the game without taking chances. The teams that struggle are not the ones that take risks. They are the ones that take the wrong risks at the wrong time.

Money works the same way.

Most athletes are not afraid of risk. You have spent years competing in high-pressure environments where outcomes were uncertain and mistakes were public. The issue is not willingness to take risk. The issue is understanding which risks are worth taking, which risks are unnecessary, and how timing changes everything.

This chapter is about awareness. Seeing the field. Knowing when to dodge hard and when to move the ball. Smart decision-making keeps possession and creates scoring opportunities. Poor risk awareness leads to turnovers.

Opening Story From the Field

Every lacrosse player recognizes this moment.

You beat your defender topside. The slide comes early. You have two options. Try to split through contact and force a shot, or move the ball to the open teammate you just created.

Forcing the shot feels aggressive. It feels confident. Sometimes it works. Often it leads to a turnover or a low-percentage attempt that hands possession back to the other team.

Great players know this is not about courage. It is about awareness. The right play depends on the situation, the score, the clock, and the personnel on the field.

Financial decisions work the same way. Risk is not good or bad on its own. Context determines whether it helps you or hurts you.

Emotional Risk vs Financial Risk

Athletes are conditioned to push through discomfort.

Fatigue.

Pain.

Pressure.

Crowd noise.

That mindset builds toughness on the field. Off the field, it can blur important distinctions.

Emotional risk is how something feels.

Financial risk is what it actually does to your future.

Chasing a hot investment may feel exciting or urgent. Avoiding a necessary expense may feel safe. Those emotions are not reliable indicators of good decisions.

In lacrosse terms, emotional risk is dodging because you feel confident. Financial risk is dodging into a double team with no outlet.

Confidence without awareness leads to turnovers.

Time Horizon Changes Everything

Risk is inseparable from time.

A risky dodge late in the shot clock is different from a risky dodge early in the possession. A gamble down by three is different from a gamble when protecting a lead.

Financially, time horizon matters just as much.

If you need money soon, volatility becomes dangerous. If you do not need money for years, short-term swings matter less. The same investment can be appropriate in one situation and reckless in another.

In lacrosse terms, this is game management.

You play differently in the first quarter than you do in the fourth. You adjust risk based on score, momentum, and remaining time.

Smart money decisions respect timing.

Flexibility Is a Form of Defense

Good offenses maintain spacing.

Spacing creates options. Options reduce forced decisions. When the field is spaced well, you can dodge with confidence because you know where help is.

Financial flexibility works the same way.

Cash reserves.

Low fixed expenses.

Manageable debt.

Transferable skills.

These create space. Space gives you options when things change. Without flexibility, even small problems force bad decisions.

Taking risk without flexibility is like dodging with no outlets. You might beat your man, but you have nowhere to go next.

How Risk Shows Up in Every Money Decision

Risk is not limited to investing.

Career decisions carry risk.

Housing choices carry risk.

Debt carries risk.

Lifestyle choices carry risk.

Overspending early limits future options.

Underinsuring exposes you to catastrophic loss.

Avoiding all risk can leave you stuck.

Risk awareness means understanding tradeoffs, not avoiding action.

In lacrosse terms, this is field IQ. Knowing that every decision shifts pressure somewhere else.

Knowing When to Dodge and When to Pass

The best offensive players are unpredictable because they are patient.

They dodge when the defense is vulnerable.

They pass when the slide commits.

They reset when nothing is there.

Financially, discipline looks the same.

You invest aggressively when time and flexibility allow.

You protect capital when stability matters.

You wait when information is incomplete.

Forcing action is rarely rewarded long term.

In lacrosse, forcing dodges leads to turnovers.

In money, forcing decisions leads to regret.

Coach's Perspective

A coach would say it plainly.

"See the field."

"Value possession."

"Make the simple play."

"Don't force it."

"Next opportunity."

Smart teams do not confuse activity with progress. They understand that keeping possession creates more chances to score.

Risk awareness is not passive. It is controlled aggression.

Game Situations and Decision Points

Situation one:

You receive unexpected income. Do you spend immediately, invest aggressively, or pause and assess how this fits your long-term plan?

Financially, this mirrors a transition opportunity. Do you force a shot or pull it out and set the offense?

Situation two:

Markets drop sharply. Do you panic and sell, freeze and do nothing, or evaluate whether this changes your long-term strategy?

This is defensive pressure. Do you rush a pass or stay composed?

Situation three:

You feel behind financially. Do you chase higher risk hoping to catch up, or tighten fundamentals and rebuild consistency?

This is late-game temptation. Do you hero dodge or trust the system?

Each decision is about risk awareness, not bravery.

Common Athlete Mistakes and Financial Parallels

Athletes force dodges when tired.

Financially, that looks like chasing returns under pressure.

Athletes confuse confidence with vision.

Financially, that leads to overconfidence and concentrated risk.

Athletes ignore spacing.

Financially, that shows up as no emergency fund or flexibility.

The same mistakes cost possession on the field and stability off it.

Winning the Long Game

Championship offenses are patient.

They win by keeping possession, moving the ball, and waiting for high-quality opportunities. They understand that not every dodge has to end in a shot.

Financial success works the same way.

Risk awareness allows you to stay aggressive without being reckless. It allows you to grow without putting everything at risk. It keeps you in control when others panic.

You do not win by forcing plays.

You win by making the right play, over and over, across a long season.

Athlete Takeaways

- See the field before you dodge. Awareness beats emotion.
- Risk changes with time, score, and situation.
- Flexibility creates space and better options.
- Forcing plays leads to turnovers.
- Smart decisions keep possession and win long seasons.

Chapter 7: Insurance Fundamentals Every Player Needs

In lacrosse, defense is not optional.

You can have elite scorers, a dominant faceoff unit, and a lethal man-up, but if you cannot protect the goal, none of it matters. One missed slide. One blown assignment. One injury without coverage behind it. The entire game changes.

Insurance plays that same role in your financial life.

It is not exciting. It does not show up on highlight reels. But when something goes wrong, insurance is what keeps one bad moment from becoming a season-ending loss. This chapter is about understanding the basic defensive schemes every athlete needs once the uniform comes off.

Opening Story From the Field

Every player remembers a defensive breakdown.

You are in good position. The ball moves quickly. One slide comes late. The offense finds the open man on the crease. Goal. Suddenly momentum flips, not because the offense was unstoppable, but because the defense was unprepared for one rotation.

Insurance exists for the same reason slides exist.

You hope you never need them. But when pressure hits, you better know who is responsible and where the help is coming from.

Most athletes do not lose financially because of poor investing. They lose because of one uncovered event. One injury. One accident. One unexpected bill that forces everything else to unravel.

Defense matters.

Health Insurance: Protecting the Most Important Asset

Your body is your first asset.

Health insurance covers medical care, prescriptions, hospital visits, and preventive services. Without it, a single injury or illness can create massive financial damage.

Athletes often underestimate this risk because they are used to team coverage. Once that disappears, the responsibility shifts entirely to you.

In lacrosse terms, health insurance is your on-ball defender.

It is the first line of defense. If it fails or is missing, everything behind it gets exposed.

Key concepts matter:

- **Premium** is what you pay to have coverage.
- **Deductible** is what you pay before insurance kicks in.
- **Out-of-pocket maximum** is the most you pay in a year.

Lower premiums often mean higher deductibles. Higher premiums often mean better coverage. There is no perfect option. The right choice depends on income, health, and risk tolerance.

Ignoring health insurance is like playing without a goalie. You might survive for a while. Eventually, it catches up.

Auto and Renters Insurance: Basic Team Defense

Auto insurance protects you when driving. Renters insurance protects your belongings and provides liability coverage if someone is injured in your space.

Both are foundational.

Auto insurance is legally required in most places. Renters insurance is often optional, which is why many athletes skip it. That is a mistake.

In lacrosse terms, auto and renters insurance are your adjacent slides.

They are not the star defenders, but they close gaps. They prevent small mistakes from becoming big goals.

Renters insurance is inexpensive and covers far more than people realize. Theft. Fire. Water damage. Liability. Skipping it to save a few dollars creates unnecessary exposure.

Defense starts with fundamentals.

Homeowners Insurance: Long-Term Defensive Responsibility

Homeowners insurance is different.

When you own property, you take on more responsibility. Structure. Liability. Weather risk. Maintenance.

Homeowners insurance protects:

- The physical structure
- Personal belongings
- Liability if someone is injured
- Additional living expenses if the home becomes unlivable

In lacrosse terms, this is your settled defense.

Once you are set, you still need discipline. One lapse creates exposure. Homeowners insurance is not just about replacing property. It is about protecting your balance sheet from catastrophic loss.

Owning without proper coverage is like leaving the crease unattended.

Deductibles, Premiums, and Coverage Limits: Understanding the Scheme

Insurance is a system, not a product.

- **Premiums** are the cost to stay in the game.
- **Deductibles** determine how much contact you absorb before help arrives.
- **Coverage limits** define how much protection you actually have.

Choosing insurance is not about minimizing premiums. It is about matching coverage to risk.

In lacrosse terms, this is scheme selection.

Aggressive defense creates turnovers but exposes the backside.

Conservative defense limits damage but requires patience.

You choose based on personnel and situation.

High deductibles lower premiums but require cash reserves.

Low deductibles increase premiums but reduce volatility.

Ignoring these tradeoffs leads to defensive breakdowns.

Common Insurance Mistakes Athletes Make

Athletes tend to make predictable mistakes.

They underinsure to save money.

They assume nothing bad will happen.

They misunderstand what is actually covered.

They never update coverage as life changes.

In lacrosse terms, this is running the wrong defense against the wrong opponent.

Life changes matter.

New job.

New location.

New assets.

New responsibilities.

Your insurance should evolve as your life evolves.

Coach's Perspective

A coach would not sugarcoat this.

"Defense wins games."

"Do your job."

"Know your assignment."

"No excuses."

"Protect the goal."

Insurance is not pessimism. It is preparation.

Great teams plan for mistakes. Great financial plans do the same.

Game Situations and Decision Points

Situation one:

You are healthy and young. Do you choose the cheapest health plan available or evaluate worst-case scenarios?

This is early-game defense. Do you get lazy or stay disciplined?

Situation two:

You rent an apartment with valuable equipment and electronics. Do you skip renters insurance because nothing has happened yet?

That is ignoring the weak-side slide.

Situation three:

You buy a home. Do you rely on minimum coverage or reassess your entire defensive setup?

That is moving from transition defense to settled defense.

Each decision is about risk management, not fear.

Common Athlete Mistakes and Financial Parallels

Athletes ball-watch.

Financially, that means focusing on investing while ignoring protection.

Athletes assume teammates will cover for them.

Financially, that means assuming nothing bad will happen.

Athletes fail to communicate on defense.

Financially, that means not understanding policies or coverage limits.

The same habits show up everywhere.

Winning the Long Game

Insurance does not help you win today's game.

It keeps you eligible to play the rest of the season.

One uncovered event can undo years of progress. Solid protection allows you to stay aggressive elsewhere because your downside is controlled.

Championship teams protect the goal first.

Financially strong athletes do the same.

Athlete Takeaways

- Defense is not optional. Insurance protects your entire game.
- Health insurance is your first and most important defender.
- Auto, renters, and homeowners coverage close gaps before damage spreads.
- Premiums, deductibles, and limits are scheme decisions, not guesses.
- Protect the goal so one bad play does not end the season.

Chapter 8: Life, Disability, and Liability Protection

In lacrosse, great teams plan for more than the next possession.

They prepare for injuries, foul trouble, weather shifts, and momentum swings. Coaches build depth charts because availability is never guaranteed. When a starter goes down, the system does not collapse because protection and preparation were already in place.

Life, disability, and liability coverage are your off-ball defense.

They are not exciting. They do not score goals. But when something unexpected happens, they determine whether you stay in the game or watch from the sideline while everything else unravels.

Opening Story From the Field

Every player remembers the moment a key teammate went down.

It is never part of the plan. A non-contact injury. An awkward collision. Suddenly the rotation changes. The offense has to adjust. The defense has to cover more ground. Teams that prepared survive. Teams that relied on hope scramble.

Financial protection works the same way.

You do not buy coverage because you expect something bad to happen. You buy it because the game is physical, unpredictable, and long. Protection is how you stay available.

Term vs Permanent Life Insurance

Life insurance exists to protect people who depend on you.

If your absence would create financial hardship for someone else, life insurance matters. If no one relies on your income yet, it may not be a priority. The purpose is protection, not complexity.

Term life insurance covers you for a specific period of time. It is straightforward, affordable, and designed to protect income during key seasons of life like starting a career, raising a family, or paying off a mortgage.

Permanent life insurance lasts your entire life and includes additional features like cash value. It costs more and requires careful planning.

In lacrosse terms, term insurance is your reliable short-stick defender. Simple. Efficient. Gets the job done.

Permanent insurance is a specialty long-stick package. Useful in the right system, but not something you install before mastering fundamentals.

Most athletes early in their financial lives need clean, basic protection. Overcomplicating coverage too early is like installing advanced sets before learning to cradle under pressure.

Disability Insurance and Income Protection

This is one of the most overlooked protections for athletes.

You insure your car.

You insure your gear.

You insure your phone.

Yet many people fail to insure the one thing that produces everything else. Their ability to earn income.

Disability insurance replaces a portion of your income if injury or illness prevents you from working. It protects cash flow, not just catastrophic events.

In lacrosse terms, this is protecting possession.

If you cannot keep the ball, the offense stops. If you cannot work, the financial plan stops. Investments do not matter if income disappears.

Athletes often believe they can grind through anything. That mindset wins games. Financially, it leaves you exposed.

Disability insurance is not about expecting injury. It is about recognizing that your earning power is your most valuable asset, especially early in your career.

Umbrella Liability Coverage

Umbrella insurance provides additional liability protection on top of auto and homeowners policies.

As income and assets grow, exposure grows. One accident. One misunderstanding. One bad moment. Lawsuits are rare, but when they happen, they are expensive.

Umbrella coverage exists for worst-case scenarios.

In lacrosse terms, this is your slide package behind the slide.

You hope the primary defender holds. But when something breaks down, help defense prevents the easy goal.

Umbrella policies are relatively inexpensive for the amount of protection they provide. They are often ignored until they are desperately needed.

Protection should grow as your life grows.

How These Coverages Work Together

Life insurance protects people.

Disability insurance protects income.

Liability coverage protects assets.

They work as a unit.

In lacrosse terms, this is team defense. On-ball pressure, adjacent slides, crease protection. Each role matters. Ignoring one creates a weakness that offenses exploit.

Financial protection is not about avoiding risk entirely. It is about controlling downside so one mistake does not erase years of progress.

Common Insurance Mistakes Athletes Make

The same mistakes show up repeatedly.

Athletes assume youth equals safety.

Financially, that leads to skipping coverage.

Athletes focus only on cost.

Financially, that leads to underinsuring.

Athletes insure possessions but not income.

Financially, that leaves the most valuable asset exposed.

Athletes never update coverage.

Financially, that creates gaps as life changes.

Insurance mistakes do not show up immediately. They show up when stakes are highest and options are limited.

Coach's Perspective

A coach would be blunt.

"Protect the goal."

"Do your job."

"No shortcuts."

"Availability matters."

"Next man up only works if the depth chart is built."

Coverage is not fear. It is responsibility.

Professionals plan for contact.

Game Situations and Decision Points

Situation one:

You are single and healthy. Do you skip disability coverage or protect your income anyway?

This is choosing whether to defend before the offense attacks.

Situation two:

You get married or have kids. Do you add life insurance or assume you will figure it out later?

This is adjusting the defense when the opponent changes formation.

Situation three:

Your income grows. Do you add umbrella coverage or assume lawsuits only happen to other people?

This is trusting help defense before you need it.

These are professional decisions, not emotional ones.

Common Athlete Mistakes and Financial Parallels

Athletes underestimate injury risk.

Financially, that means no income protection.

Athletes ignore help defense.

Financially, that means no umbrella coverage.

Athletes resist adjustments.

Financially, that means outdated protection.

What costs games late also costs financial stability over time.

Winning the Long Game

You cannot control injuries, illness, or legal risk.

You can control preparation.

Life insurance protects people.

Disability insurance protects income.

Liability coverage protects everything else.

When protection is in place, you are free to play offense elsewhere. You can invest, build, and take smart risks knowing your downside is controlled.

Championship teams prepare for what they cannot control.

Financially disciplined athletes do the same.

Athlete Takeaways

- Protect people, income, and assets like you protect the goal.
- Term life is fundamentals. Specialty coverage comes later.
- Disability insurance protects possession when you cannot play.
- Umbrella coverage is help defense for worst-case scenarios.
- Preparation keeps you available for the long season.

Part III: Building the Offense (Investing Fundamentals)

Ball movement creates scoring opportunities.

Great lacrosse offenses do not rely on one dodger forcing shots. They move the ball. They stretch the defense. They create advantages through patience, spacing, and timing. The goal is not to score on the first touch. The goal is to create the best possible look by making the defense work.

Investing works the same way.

This part of the book is about offense. Not reckless offense. Not hero ball. Controlled, repeatable offense built on fundamentals. The kind that produces results over an entire season, not just a highlight or two.

Offense Is About Structure, Not Speed

Young players often confuse speed with effectiveness.

They sprint into dodges without reading the slide. They shoot because the clock is running, not because the look is good. It feels aggressive, but it is inefficient.

Investing has the same trap.

Fast decisions feel productive. Constant action feels like engagement. In reality, unnecessary movement creates mistakes. Good investing is not about doing more. It is about doing the right things consistently.

In lacrosse terms, this is offensive discipline.

You move the ball with purpose.

You understand where the defense is vulnerable.

You wait for the right window instead of forcing contact.

Possession Matters More Than Shots

The best offenses value possession.

They protect the ball. They avoid turnovers. They understand that every extra pass increases the chance of a breakdown somewhere else on the field.

Financially, possession is ownership.

Owning productive assets over time is what creates growth. Jumping in and out of markets, chasing trends, or reacting to noise is the equivalent of throwing risky passes across the middle. Sometimes it works. Over time, it costs you games.

This part of the book focuses on:

- Understanding what you actually own
- Why different assets play different roles
- How time and discipline turn small advantages into big outcomes

Offense starts with keeping the ball.

Efficiency Beats Power

In lacrosse, goals do not care how hard you shoot.

They care where the ball goes.

A well-placed shot beats raw power every time. The same principle applies to investing. You do not need extreme risk to succeed. You need efficiency. Tax efficiency. Cost efficiency. Behavioral efficiency.

Small leaks add up.

High fees matter.

Poor timing matters.

Emotional decisions matter.

Efficient offense wears defenses down.

Efficient investing does the same thing to financial goals.

Market Movement Is Not the Enemy

Many athletes struggle with investing because they misunderstand movement.

They see volatility as danger.

They see pullbacks as failure.

They see quiet periods as wasted time.

In lacrosse, movement is constant.

Momentum swings.

Runs happen.

Games tighten.

Then they open back up.

You do not abandon the offense because the other team scores twice. You reset. You execute. You trust the system.

Markets behave the same way.

This part will teach you how to:

- Understand market cycles without trying to predict them
- Separate normal movement from real risk
- Stay invested when emotions tell you to force plays

Calm offense beats frantic defense.

Why Fundamentals Matter More Than Talent

Some athletes enter investing thinking talent will carry them.

They are smart.

They work hard.

They assume they will figure it out as they go.

That approach fails in both sports and money.

Fundamentals matter more than confidence.

Systems matter more than instincts.

Consistency matters more than intensity.

This section is not about shortcuts.

It is about building an offense you can run under pressure.

What This Part Will Give You

By the end of Part III, you should understand:

- How financial markets actually function
- What stocks, bonds, and funds really do
- Why patience creates advantage
- How to think long term without losing edge

You are not learning plays to impress anyone.

You are learning how to score repeatedly without turning the ball over.

Coach's Perspective

A coach would keep it simple.

"Move the ball."

"Value possession."

"Make the defense work."

"Don't force shots."

"Trust the system."

Offense is about discipline.

So is investing.

Building a great offense takes time.

You do not master it in one practice.

You do not perfect it in one game.

You earn it through reps, film, adjustments, and patience.

That is what this part is about.

Ball movement.

Vision.

Execution.

Score by doing the simple things well, over and over, until the defense breaks.

Chapter 9: How Financial Markets Really Work

Lacrosse players learn early that the game looks chaotic until you understand spacing.

At full speed, the ball is flying. Players are cutting. Slides are coming from unexpected angles. To someone new, it looks random. To an experienced player, it is structured. You see the rotations. You anticipate the slide. You know where the next pass should go before it happens.

Financial markets feel the same way.

To people outside the system, markets look unpredictable. Prices move every day. Headlines scream urgency. Opinions flood in from every direction. It feels noisy and emotional. But underneath the surface is structure. Once you understand how markets actually function, the chaos slows down.

This chapter is about learning to see the field.

Opening Story From the Field

Every experienced lacrosse player remembers the moment the game slowed down.

Early on, everything feels rushed. You cradle too tight. You force dodges. You rush shots because you feel pressure even when there is space. Over time, reps change that. You begin to recognize patterns. You stop reacting and start anticipating.

The game does not slow down.

You do.

That same shift happens when athletes truly understand financial markets. The noise never goes away. Your ability to process it does.

How Financial Markets Function

At their core, financial markets exist to connect people who need capital with people willing to provide it.

Companies raise money to grow.

Governments borrow to fund projects.

Investors supply that capital in exchange for ownership or repayment.

Prices move based on expectations about the future, not just what is happening today. That is the part many athletes miss. Markets are forward-looking. They react before outcomes are fully known.

In lacrosse terms, the market is the field itself.

Teams compete.

Some rebuild.

Some dominate.

Others struggle.

Standings change, but the season keeps moving.

Markets are not designed to feel comfortable. They are designed to function. Volatility is not a flaw. It is part of how information gets processed.

When athletes panic during market movement, it is usually because they mistake motion for danger.

Stocks, Bonds, and Ownership

Understanding markets starts with understanding ownership.

Stocks represent ownership in a company. When you buy a stock, you own a piece of a real business. You participate in its growth, profits, and setbacks. Stock prices move daily, but underneath the price is a company selling products, paying employees, and trying to grow.

Bonds are loans. You lend money to a government or company and receive interest in return. The upside is lower, but the structure is more stable.

In lacrosse terms:

- Stocks are your primary dodgers and scorers. They create opportunity but experience runs and cold streaks.
- Bonds are your defenders and short-stick midfielders. They do not grab headlines, but they stabilize the game.

A winning team needs both offense and defense. A strong portfolio works the same way.

Investing is not betting.

It is ownership over time.

Market Cycles and Volatility

Markets move in cycles.

Growth.

Slowdowns.

Pullbacks.

Recoveries.

This is normal.

Volatility is movement, not failure. Prices moving up and down does not mean something is broken. It means expectations are changing.

In lacrosse terms, this is momentum.

No team dominates every quarter.

Runs happen.

Games tighten.

Then they open back up.

Athletes who abandon the offense after one bad possession make the same mistake investors make when they panic during volatility.

The market's job is not to be smooth.

Its job is to reflect changing conditions.

Volatility becomes dangerous only when emotion turns movement into poor decisions.

Long-Term Strategy vs Forcing Plays

One of the biggest mistakes athletes make with money is forcing plays.

They chase what is hot.

They react to headlines.

They jump in and out trying to time perfect moments.

In lacrosse terms, this is dodging into traffic with no plan.

Sometimes it works.

Over time, it costs you possession.

Long-term investing is about system execution, not hero moments. It is about staying invested, letting compounding work, and trusting time rather than instinct.

Good offenses take what the defense gives them.

Good investors take what the market offers without forcing outcomes.

The goal is not to win every possession.

The goal is to win the game.

Why Markets Feel Emotional to Athletes

Athletes are wired for action.

You are trained to respond.

To adjust quickly.

To compete every rep.

Markets punish overreaction.

The skills that win games can hurt investment results if they are not controlled. Discipline, patience, and structure matter more than speed.

In lacrosse terms, this is learning when to dodge and when to move the ball.

Not every possession requires aggression.

Some require restraint.

Understanding this shift is what separates disciplined investors from reactive ones.

Coach's Perspective

A coach would not overcomplicate this.

"See the whole field."

"Value possession."

"Don't force shots."

"Trust the offense."

"One possession at a time."

Markets reward execution, not emotion.

The athletes who succeed financially are the ones who treat investing like a season, not a highlight reel.

Game Situations and Decision Points

Situation one:

The market drops sharply. Do you panic and sell, or do you recognize a normal cycle and stay disciplined?

This is playing through a defensive run without abandoning the system.

Situation two:

You hear about a hot investment from friends or social media. Do you chase it, or do you evaluate whether it fits your strategy?

This is choosing between forcing a dodge or swinging the ball.

Situation three:

Markets are calm and boring. Do you lose interest or stay consistent?

This is running offense patiently until the opening appears.

Each decision compounds over time.

Common Athlete Mistakes and Financial Parallels

Athletes rush decisions.

Financially, that leads to market timing mistakes.

Athletes chase momentum.

Financially, that leads to buying high and selling low.

Athletes abandon structure.

Financially, that leads to inconsistent results.

The same habits show up everywhere.

Winning the Long Game

Markets reward ownership, patience, and discipline.

You do not need to predict every move.

You do not need to react to every headline.

You need to stay invested and let time work.

Great lacrosse offenses score by trusting the system.

Great investors do the same.

When you understand how markets really work, the noise fades. You stop reacting. You start executing.

That is when the game slows down.

Athlete Takeaways

- Markets are structured systems, not chaos
- Stocks mean ownership, bonds mean stability
- Volatility is normal movement, not failure
- Long-term strategy beats forcing plays
- See the whole field and value possession

Chapter 10: Risk, Return, and the Power of Compounding

Every lacrosse player learns quickly that not all shots are equal.

An open step-down from the wing.

A time-and-room shot after clean ball movement.

A low-angle rip while falling away from pressure.

They all count as goals if they go in, but they do not carry the same probability. Smart players understand risk. They know when to attack, when to move the ball, and when to reset. They do not judge decisions only by outcomes. They judge them by quality.

Money works the same way.

Risk, return, and compounding are not complicated ideas. They are misunderstood because people chase outcomes instead of understanding the process. This chapter is about learning how to take smart shots repeatedly over a long season.

Opening Story From the Field

Every team has a player who forces offense.

They dodge into traffic.

They shoot early in the clock.

They try to make something happen every possession.

Sometimes it works. When it does, the crowd reacts. When it does not, the offense stalls and possession disappears.

Great teams learn a different lesson.

They understand that patience creates better looks. They accept small resets because they know the next pass might create a high-percentage opportunity.

That mindset translates directly to investing.

The goal is not to swing as hard as possible. The goal is to take the right amount of risk for the situation and let repetition do the work.

Risk and Reward Tradeoffs

There is no reward without risk.

In lacrosse, attacking the middle creates scoring chances, but it also brings contact. Playing safe all game limits turnovers, but it also limits offense. Coaches constantly balance risk and reward based on time, score, and personnel.

Financially, the same tradeoff exists.

Higher potential returns usually come with higher risk. Lower-risk investments tend to be more stable but grow more slowly. There is no perfect option that delivers high returns with no downside.

In lacrosse terms, this is shot selection.

You do not take contested shots every possession. You mix dodges, ball movement, and spacing based on what the defense gives you. Smart investing is about matching risk to your situation, not chasing the biggest possible upside.

Risk is not the enemy.

Unmanaged risk is.

Volatility vs Permanent Loss

This is where many athletes get tripped up.

Volatility is movement.

Permanent loss is damage.

Markets going up and down is normal. That movement feels uncomfortable, especially when account values drop. But volatility alone does not mean something is broken.

Permanent loss happens when you panic, overextend, or abandon discipline.

In lacrosse terms, volatility is missing a few shots.

Permanent loss is turning the ball over repeatedly and giving up transition goals.

One is part of the game.

The other changes outcomes.

Athletes often mistake discomfort for danger. Seeing numbers go down feels like failure even when the long-term plan is intact. Understanding this difference is critical.

You cannot avoid volatility.

You can avoid decisions that turn volatility into permanent damage.

The Power of Compounding Over Time

Compounding is growth built on growth.

Your money earns returns.

Those returns earn returns.

Over time, the effect accelerates.

This is not about brilliance. It is about repetition.

In lacrosse terms, compounding is possession time.

One extra pass does not seem meaningful. Over an entire game, possession wears defenses down. Over a season, it separates disciplined teams from impatient ones.

Compounding works the same way financially.

Early progress feels slow.

Then momentum builds.

Then growth becomes noticeable.

Time is the multiplier. The earlier you start, the more powerful compounding becomes. Not because you are smarter, but because you give the process more reps.

Consistency beats intensity.

Why Time Matters More Than Timing

Athletes love timing.

You wait for the perfect cut.

You attack when the slide is late.

You finish when the goalie is out of position.

In investing, people try to apply the same instinct.

They wait for the perfect entry.

They wait for the bottom.

They wait until things feel safe.

The problem is that time keeps moving.

Every year you wait is a year compounding cannot work for you. That lost time cannot be recovered.

In lacrosse terms, this is refusing to shoot open looks because you are waiting for the perfect one. Eventually, the clock runs out.

You do not need perfect timing.

You need time in the game.

The Hidden Cost of Waiting

Waiting feels responsible.

It feels cautious.

It feels smart.

It is often expensive.

Delaying investing means missing years of compounding. Even small contributions started early often outperform larger contributions started late.

In lacrosse terms, skipping offseason training puts you behind before the season starts. You can still compete, but you are chasing instead of building.

You do not need to start big.

You do need to start.

Matching Risk to Your Season of Life

Risk is not static.

Early in your career, time is on your side. Volatility matters less because recovery time is long. Growth-oriented strategies often make sense.

As responsibilities increase and timelines shorten, stability becomes more important. Risk still exists, but it is managed differently.

In lacrosse terms, this is adjusting game plans as the season progresses.

Young teams run more.

Veteran teams control tempo.

Neither is better. They are situational.

The mistake is playing the wrong style for your stage.

Coach's Perspective

A coach would make this simple.

"Take good shots."

"Trust the reps."

"Do not force it."

"Play the long game."

"Finish strong."

Risk is part of competition.

Discipline determines outcomes.

Game Situations and Decision Points

Situation one:

The market drops sharply. Do you stop investing or keep showing up?

This is playing through a scoring drought without abandoning the offense.

Situation two:

You feel behind financially. Do you force risk or stay disciplined?

This is taking contested shots because you want points quickly.

Situation three:

You want to wait for the perfect moment. Do you start anyway?

This is choosing whether to shoot an open look or let the clock expire.

Each decision compounds.

Common Athlete Mistakes and Financial Parallels

Athletes chase quick goals.

Financially, that leads to excessive risk.

Athletes fear mistakes.

Financially, that leads to inactivity.

Athletes confuse effort with strategy.

Financially, that leads to burnout.

The habits that cost possessions cost money too.

Winning the Long Game

Compounding does not reward excitement.

It rewards consistency.

Risk is unavoidable.

Volatility is normal.

Time is powerful.

Stay invested.

Stay disciplined.

Keep taking quality shots.

Over time, small advantages stack into meaningful results.

Great lacrosse teams win by controlling possession and trusting the system.

Great investors do the same.

Athlete Takeaways

- Risk and reward always move together
- Volatility is normal, permanent loss is avoidable
- Compounding rewards reps and patience
- Waiting costs more than starting imperfectly
- Take good shots consistently and trust the long game

Chapter 11: Stocks Without the Hero Ball

Every lacrosse player has seen hero ball.

One player dodges from the top every possession. They take shots through double teams. Sometimes it works and the crowd reacts. Over time, possessions disappear, teammates disengage, and the offense stalls. Coaches tolerate it briefly. They never build championships around it.

Stocks get treated the same way.

People chase the one company that will change everything. The hot name. The overnight winner. The stock that is supposed to score from anywhere on the field. This chapter slows the game down and replaces hero ball with disciplined offense.

Opening Story From the Field

Think about the best offense you ever played on.

The ball moved. Cuts were timed. Shots came from advantage, not desperation. No one needed to force anything because everyone trusted the system.

Now think about the opposite.

One player holds the ball. The defense loads up. The shot clock runs down. A tough shot goes up. Sometimes it drops. Most of the time it does not.

The difference was not talent.

It was decision-making.

That same difference separates disciplined stock investors from hype chasers.

What Owning Stock Actually Means

Buying a stock is not betting on a ticker.

It is owning a piece of a real business.

When you own stock, you own a share of a company that sells products or services, hires employees, competes in an industry, and tries to grow profits over time. The stock price moves daily, but the business underneath moves much slower.

In lacrosse terms, owning stock is being part of the offense, not just watching highlights.

You are on the field for good possessions and bad ones. You stay engaged through runs, droughts, and adjustments. Ownership requires patience and understanding.

If you do not know what the company does, how it makes money, or why it should exist long term, you are not investing. You are forcing shots.

Growth vs Value Investing

Stocks generally fall into different styles. Two of the most common are growth and value.

Growth investing focuses on companies expected to expand quickly. Revenue is rising. Markets are expanding. Expectations are high. Prices often reflect optimism about the future, which means volatility is higher.

Value investing focuses on companies that appear inexpensive relative to their fundamentals. Growth may be slower. Businesses are often mature. Prices are lower because expectations are more conservative.

Neither approach is right or wrong.

In lacrosse terms, growth stocks are fast-break offense. They create excitement, momentum, and runs. Value stocks are settled offense. They work the ball, protect possession, and score efficiently.

Problems show up when you expect one style to behave like the other.

Fast-break teams struggle in slow games.

Settled offenses do not win sprint contests.

Smart investors understand roles. They do not panic when growth cools or value moves quietly. They build lineups that include both and let each play its part.

Dividends and Total Return

Dividends confuse a lot of athletes.

Dividends are cash payments companies make to shareholders. They are not free money. They are part of total return.

Total return includes:

- Price changes
- Dividends received
- Reinvested earnings over time

In lacrosse terms, total return is the final score.

Goals matter.

Assists matter.

Possession matters.

Defense matters.

Focusing only on dividends is like focusing only on assists. Focusing only on price is like focusing only on goals. You need the whole picture.

Some companies pay dividends. Others reinvest profits to grow faster. Both approaches can work. What matters is how the entire system performs over time.

Why Stocks Feel Emotional

Stocks move every day.

Prices rise. Prices fall. News hits. Opinions spread. That movement triggers emotion, especially for competitive people who are wired to react.

Athletes struggle with stocks because they confuse action with effectiveness.

In lacrosse, not every possession requires a dodge. Sometimes the best play is moving the ball and letting the defense shift.

In investing, not every movement requires a response. Constant trading creates friction, taxes, and mistakes. Ownership rewards patience, not reaction.

Common Investing Myths Athletes Fall For

A few myths show up repeatedly.

Myth: Stocks are gambling

Reality: Ownership with discipline is investing. Guessing without a plan is gambling.

Myth: You need to pick winners

Reality: Diversification and consistency matter more than finding the next star.

Myth: Aggression wins

Reality: Discipline wins more games than forced shots.

Myth: You can time the market

Reality: Most people cannot, and trying often hurts results.

These myths persist because they feel competitive. Lacrosse teaches you that fundamentals beat flash over a season.

Stocks as Part of a System

Stocks are offense.

They drive growth. They create opportunity. They also miss shots.

A portfolio built only on stocks without balance is like running six attackers and no defense. It can work briefly. It collapses under pressure.

Stocks belong inside a broader system that includes defense, flexibility, and time horizon. When used correctly, they are powerful. When forced, they create volatility you cannot emotionally handle.

Coach's Perspective

A coach would be direct.

"Move the ball."

"Trust the offense."

"Do not force shots."

"Play within the system."

"Value possession."

Hero ball loses games.

Discipline wins seasons.

Game Situations and Decision Points

Situation one:

You hear about a hot stock from friends or social media. Do you research the business and its role in your lineup, or do you chase momentum?

This is choosing between a forced dodge and an extra pass.

Situation two:

A stock you own drops sharply. Do you panic and sell, or do you reassess fundamentals?

This is staying composed after a defensive run.

Situation three:

You want excitement. Do you sacrifice discipline for entertainment?

This is playing for the crowd instead of the scoreboard.

Each choice compounds.

Common Athlete Mistakes and Financial Parallels

Athletes force offense.

Financially, that leads to hype investing.

Athletes ignore roles.

Financially, that leads to unbalanced portfolios.

Athletes overreact to mistakes.

Financially, that leads to buying high and selling low.

The habits are the same.

Winning the Long Game

Stocks reward ownership, patience, and understanding.

You do not need to be perfect.

You do not need to be flashy.

You need to stay disciplined.

Great lacrosse offenses score by trusting the system.

Great investors do the same.

Hero ball feels exciting.

Disciplined offense wins championships.

Athlete Takeaways

- Owning stock means owning a business, not chasing a name
- Growth and value play different roles in the offense
- Dividends are part of total return, not free points
- Forcing plays creates turnovers in investing too
- Move the ball, trust the system, and let time work

Chapter 12: Bonds and Staying Balanced

Not every goal in lacrosse comes from a fast break.

Some games are won by patience, positioning, and controlling tempo. When the game tightens, when legs get heavy, and when emotions run hot, the teams that stay balanced survive. They value possession. They play defense. They understand that slowing the game down is sometimes the smartest move.

Bonds play that role in a financial plan.

They are not exciting. They do not dominate headlines. But when conditions get rough, bonds are what keep the entire system from tipping over. This chapter is about understanding why balance matters and why defense is just as important as offense.

Opening Story From the Field

Every lacrosse player remembers a game where speed stopped working.

The other team figured out your transition.

The field got muddy.

Officials tightened the whistle.

Momentum swung back and forth.

Suddenly, the game slowed down.

Teams that relied only on speed and aggression struggled. Teams that could settle the ball, work the offense, and protect defensively stayed composed. They did not panic. They trusted fundamentals.

Bonds exist for the same reason.

When markets slow, tighten, or turn volatile, bonds provide structure that allows you to stay in the game without emotional mistakes.

How Bonds Work

At their core, bonds are loans.

You lend money to a government or a company. In return, you receive interest payments, and your original principal is returned at maturity, assuming the borrower does not default.

Unlike stocks, bonds do not represent ownership. They represent a contractual obligation.

In lacrosse terms, bonds are defensive possessions.

You are not trying to score quickly. You are trying to control the game, limit mistakes, and protect field position. Bonds are designed to provide income and stability, not explosive growth.

Bond values can move, but their role is different. They exist to smooth volatility and create reliability.

Defense is a choice. So is bond exposure.

Interest Rate Risk and Credit Risk

Two main risks affect bonds.

Interest rate risk means bond prices move when interest rates change. When rates rise, existing bonds become less attractive. When rates fall, existing bonds become more valuable.

Credit risk is the risk that the borrower cannot repay the loan.

In lacrosse terms, interest rate risk is pace.

When the game speeds up, some lineups struggle. When it slows down, others gain an advantage.

Credit risk is matchup.

A short-stick defender may thrive against one dodger and struggle against another. The quality of the matchup matters.

Higher bond yields usually mean higher risk. There is no free lunch. Just like defense, discipline and awareness matter.

Why Bonds Feel Boring but Matter

Athletes often undervalue bonds because they do not feel productive.

Stocks move.

Prices change.

Excitement exists.

Bonds feel quiet.

In lacrosse terms, this is ignoring defense because goals feel better than stops.

Defense does not feel exciting. It feels necessary when the game tightens. Bonds play the same role financially. They reduce volatility, provide income, and create flexibility during market stress.

Without bonds, portfolios often become emotionally unmanageable. Athletes panic when markets drop because they have no ballast.

Balance prevents panic.

When Bonds Make Sense

Bonds make sense when stability matters.

As income grows.

As responsibilities increase.

As timelines shorten.

As emotional tolerance for volatility decreases.

Early in your career, time is your biggest asset. Volatility matters less. Growth assets often dominate.

Later, stability becomes more important.

In lacrosse terms, this is lineup management.

Young teams push pace.

Veteran teams control tempo.

Both styles win when used intentionally. The mistake is running a fast-break offense when the game calls for patience.

Bonds are not about fear.

They are about situational awareness.

Bonds in a Diversified Portfolio

Bonds are not designed to replace stocks.

They complement them.

A diversified portfolio needs offense and defense. Bonds reduce swings, generate income, and provide dry powder during downturns. That stability allows you to stay invested rather than react emotionally.

In lacrosse terms, bonds are your short-stick midfielders.

They may not score often. But they are always in the right place. They transition the ball. They prevent easy goals. They keep the system functioning.

Ignoring bonds completely is like playing six attackers and hoping the other team never counters.

Common Bond Misunderstandings

Athletes often misunderstand bonds.

They assume bonds never lose value.

They assume bonds are always safe.

They assume bonds are unnecessary if they are young.

All three are wrong.

Bonds carry risk.

Bonds fluctuate.

Bonds serve specific roles.

The question is not whether bonds are good or bad. The question is whether your portfolio can handle pressure without them.

Emotional Benefits of Bonds

One of the biggest advantages of bonds is behavioral.

They reduce volatility.

They smooth returns.

They help you stay disciplined.

Athletes often underestimate how emotion affects money decisions. Bonds act like a calming presence on the field. When chaos hits, they allow you to slow down and make rational decisions.

In lacrosse terms, this is the veteran who settles everyone during a run.

That presence matters.

Coach's Perspective

A coach would emphasize balance.

"Protect the goal."

"Control tempo."

"Stay disciplined."

"Do not chase."

"Finish strong."

Defense travels.

So does financial stability.

Game Situations and Decision Points

Situation one:

Markets become volatile. Do you panic, or do you rely on balance to stay composed?

That is choosing discipline over emotion.

Situation two:

You need money in the near future. Do you chase returns or protect capital?

That is recognizing time and score.

Situation three:

You feel bored with steady returns. Do you abandon balance or trust the system?

That is resisting the urge to force offense.

Each decision affects the entire season.

Common Athlete Mistakes and Financial Parallels

Athletes undervalue defense.

Financially, that means ignoring bonds.

Athletes chase speed constantly.

Financially, that means excessive risk.

Athletes forget situational awareness.

Financially, that leads to poor timing.

The habits that lose games lose money too.

Winning the Long Game

Championship teams are balanced.

They score when opportunities appear.

They defend when pressure rises.

They adjust without panic.

Bonds help you do the same financially.

They slow the game down.

They reduce mistakes.

They give you options.

You do not win championships on offense alone.

You do not build financial stability without defense.

Athlete Takeaways

- Bonds are defensive possessions that protect field position
- Interest rate and credit risk are pace and matchup decisions
- Bonds matter more as timelines shorten and pressure increases
- Balance reduces volatility and emotional mistakes
- Great teams and strong portfolios win by staying composed

Chapter 13: Funds, ETFs, and Team-Based Investing

Lacrosse is not a solo sport.

Even the best dodger in the world cannot beat six defenders every possession. Championships are won by ball movement, spacing, timing, and trust. When everyone understands their role and the ball moves faster than any one player, the offense becomes hard to stop.

Funds and ETFs work the same way.

They are team-based investing. Instead of relying on one stock, one idea, or one prediction, you spread responsibility across many players. That approach reduces risk, increases consistency, and allows you to stay in the game through long seasons without forcing plays.

This chapter is about building an offense that works together.

Opening Story From the Field

Think about the best offensive unit you were ever part of.

The ball rarely stuck in one player's stick. Cuts were sharp. Passes were on time. Shots came from advantage, not desperation. Everyone knew the system, and no one needed to be the hero.

Now think about the opposite.

One player dominates possession. Teammates stop cutting. The defense loads up. Turnovers increase. Even if that player is talented, the offense becomes predictable.

That same dynamic shows up in investing.

Relying on one stock or one idea feels exciting. Over time, it creates unnecessary risk. Team-based investing creates balance and sustainability.

What Funds and ETFs Actually Are

Mutual funds and ETFs pool money from many investors and invest it across multiple securities.

Instead of buying one stock, you buy exposure to dozens, hundreds, or even thousands of companies through a single investment. The goal is not to eliminate risk. The goal is to spread it intelligently.

In lacrosse terms, this is running an offense instead of isolation.

You are still trying to score. You are just doing it through structure rather than force.

The biggest advantage of funds and ETFs is not performance. It is consistency.

Mutual Funds vs ETFs

Mutual funds and ETFs are similar, but they operate a little differently.

Mutual funds are typically bought and sold at one price per day, after the market closes. You invest a dollar amount, and everyone transacts at the same net asset value.

ETFs trade throughout the day like stocks. Prices move during market hours, and you can place different types of orders.

In lacrosse terms, both run organized systems.

Mutual funds are like settled offense. Controlled pace. Fewer decisions during the possession.

ETFs are like transition opportunities. More flexibility. More movement. More choice.

Neither is automatically better. The wrapper matters less than what is inside. What matters is the strategy, the cost, and how it fits into your overall game plan.

Index vs Active Strategies

Index strategies aim to match the performance of a market or segment. They follow rules. They do not try to outthink anyone. They are consistent and typically low cost.

Active strategies attempt to outperform the market through selection and timing. They rely on decision-making, judgment, and execution.

In lacrosse terms, index investing is running a proven offensive system. Active investing is trusting individual playmaking.

Both can work.

Problems arise when athletes expect active strategies to deliver consistent dominance without understanding how difficult that is. Even elite players miss shots. Even great dodgers get shut down by good defenses.

Most investors benefit from building around a strong system first, then adding individual playmaking carefully, if at all.

System before hero ball.

Fees and Expense Ratios

Fees matter more than most athletes realize.

Expense ratios reduce returns every year, whether performance is good or bad. They are quiet. They are automatic. And over time, they compound against you.

In lacrosse terms, fees are turnovers.

One turnover does not lose the game. Over a season, they change outcomes. High fees make winning harder without adding any extra skill or effort.

Low cost does not guarantee success.

High cost guarantees headwinds.

Great teams value efficiency. Great portfolios do too.

Diversification Without Complexity

Diversification is often misunderstood.

It does not mean owning everything.

It does not mean endless accounts.

It does not mean constant tinkering.

It means spreading risk intelligently.

Different companies.

Different sectors.

Different regions.

Different roles.

Funds and ETFs make diversification simple. One decision can give you exposure to a full roster instead of relying on a single player to do everything.

In lacrosse terms, this is roster balance.

You do not need six stars. You need players who fit together. When one option is taken away, another steps up.

Diversification reduces the impact of mistakes. It does not remove risk, but it makes risk manageable.

Why Athletes Struggle With Team-Based Investing

Athletes are trained to compete.

You want to win.

You want to be right.

You want to feel in control.

Team-based investing requires humility.

You accept market returns.

You accept that you will not always be first.

You accept that consistency beats flash.

That feels uncomfortable at first. Over time, it feels freeing.

You spend less energy reacting and more energy executing.

Funds as the Core of the Game Plan

For many athletes, funds and ETFs should form the core of the portfolio.

They provide:

- Broad exposure
- Lower costs
- Built-in diversification
- Less decision fatigue

That does not mean you never own individual stocks. It means individual decisions should complement the system, not replace it.

In lacrosse terms, this is building the offense first, then letting individual talent shine within it.

Coach's Perspective

A coach would keep it simple.

"Share the ball."

"Trust the system."

"Know your role."

"Play together."

"Win as a unit."

Team basketball wins more than isolation.

Team lacrosse does too.

So does team-based investing.

Game Situations and Decision Points

Situation one:

You want simplicity. Do you choose a diversified fund or chase individual names?

That is choosing system offense over isolation.

Situation two:

You hear about a high-fee product with big promises. Do you evaluate cost and role, or get distracted by hype?

That is reading the defense before dodging.

Situation three:

You feel bored with steady progress. Do you force plays or trust the process?

That is staying disciplined late in the game.

Each choice compounds over time.

Common Athlete Mistakes and Financial Parallels

Athletes rely on individual talent.

Financially, that leads to concentrated risk.

Athletes ignore efficiency.

Financially, that leads to high fees.

Athletes complicate execution.

Financially, that leads to confusion and inconsistency.

The same habits show up everywhere.

Winning the Long Game

Championship offenses are not built on one player.

They are built on spacing, timing, and trust. Funds and ETFs allow you to invest the same way. They reduce the need for constant decisions and help you stay consistent when emotions run high.

You do not need to outsmart the market.

You need to stay in the game.

Team-based investing is not flashy.

It works.

Athlete Takeaways

- Team offense beats hero ball in investing too
- Funds and ETFs spread risk across the whole roster
- Index strategies are systems, active strategies are playmaking
- Fees are turnovers that add up over time
- Trust the system and let the team win

Chapter 14: Real Estate and Alternative Plays

In lacrosse, not every scoring opportunity comes from the same place on the field.

Sometimes you attack from behind the goal. Sometimes you sweep topside. Sometimes the best play is to reset, draw the defense out, and attack a mismatch. Smart teams understand that variety matters. You do not run the same play every possession, and you do not rely on one angle to score.

Real estate and alternative investments work the same way.

They are not the core offense for most athletes, but they can add dimension, balance, and optionality when used correctly. Used poorly, they slow the game down, lock you into bad positions, and make adjustments difficult.

This chapter is about understanding when these plays make sense, when they do not, and how to evaluate them without forcing shots.

Opening Story From the Field

Think about a game where the defense shuts down your primary look.

Slides come early. Lanes disappear. Your first option is gone. Good teams do not panic. They move the ball, attack from a different angle, and exploit space somewhere else on the field.

Bad teams force it anyway.

They dodge into traffic. They take low-percentage shots. Possession flips, and momentum swings.

Real estate and alternatives are like secondary offensive sets.

They can be powerful when they fit the game plan. They become dangerous when athletes force them because they sound impressive or feel like the next level.

Renting vs Owning: Understanding the Role

Housing is the most common form of real estate exposure, and it is also the most misunderstood.

Renting and owning are tools, not identities.

Renting provides flexibility. Lower upfront cost. Easier exits. Fewer responsibilities. It can be the right move early in a career, during transitions, or when income is uncertain.

Owning provides stability. Potential appreciation. Forced savings through mortgage payments. It can make sense when timelines are long and cash flow is predictable.

In lacrosse terms, renting is keeping your feet moving and your stick free. Owning is setting up in a settled offense and committing to position.

The mistake athletes make is treating ownership like a trophy instead of a tool. Buying too early, stretching payments, or locking into a location that limits career flexibility is like committing to a slow dodge when the slide is already coming.

Owning a home can be a great move.

It can also be an anchor if timing is wrong.

Real Estate as an Investment

Real estate investing goes beyond personal housing.

Rental properties, multi-family units, and commercial real estate can generate income and diversify wealth. They can also introduce complexity, leverage, and risk.

Real estate requires:

- Capital
- Ongoing management
- Maintenance
- Legal and tax awareness

In lacrosse terms, this is adding a new position to your game.

You cannot just decide midseason to become a defender without learning footwork, positioning, and communication. Real estate demands reps, education, and patience.

Athletes often underestimate the work involved. Passive income is rarely passive at the beginning.

REITs and Indirect Ownership

For athletes who want real estate exposure without direct ownership, REITs offer an alternative.

Real Estate Investment Trusts own and manage properties across sectors like residential, commercial, healthcare, and industrial real estate. They trade like stocks and can be owned inside traditional investment accounts.

In lacrosse terms, REITs are like contributing to the offense without needing to carry the ball every possession.

You get exposure.

You get income.

You get diversification.

You do not get control over individual properties, but you also avoid the headaches of tenants, repairs, and leverage decisions.

REITs can be a useful complement to a portfolio, especially for athletes who value liquidity and simplicity.

Alternatives Beyond Real Estate

Alternatives include assets outside traditional stocks and bonds.

Commodities.

Private equity.

Private credit.

Hedge strategies.

Collectibles.

These investments often sound sophisticated. They are frequently marketed to athletes as exclusive opportunities.

Exclusivity is not the same as quality.

In lacrosse terms, this is being offered a trick play you have never practiced and being told it will work because no one else is running it.

Alternatives can offer diversification and return potential. They also bring:

- Complexity
- Higher fees
- Limited transparency
- Long lockups

Some alternatives belong in certain portfolios.

Many do not.

The key is understanding role, risk, and timing.

Liquidity Matters More Than Athletes Expect

Liquidity is the ability to access your money without penalty or delay.

Stocks and ETFs are liquid.

Most real estate and alternatives are not.

Once money goes into a private deal, it is often locked up for years. That can be fine if the rest of your financial life is stable. It becomes a problem if income changes, opportunities arise, or emergencies hit.

In lacrosse terms, liquidity is having an outlet pass.

If you dodge into trouble and have nowhere to move the ball, you turn it over. Illiquid investments remove flexibility. They require confidence that you will not need the money elsewhere.

Athletes often overestimate future income and underestimate how quickly situations can change.

Flexibility keeps you in control.

Leverage and Risk

Real estate often involves leverage.

Borrowing magnifies outcomes. It can accelerate growth. It can also accelerate damage.

When markets are strong and cash flow is steady, leverage feels smart. When vacancies increase or income drops, leverage turns pressure into stress.

In lacrosse terms, leverage is playing extended minutes without depth.

It works until fatigue sets in. Then mistakes multiply.

Debt tied to real assets requires discipline, reserves, and conservative assumptions. Without those, leverage becomes a liability rather than a tool.

Why Athletes Are Drawn to Alternative Plays

Athletes are competitive.

You want edges.

You want upside.

You want to feel ahead of the curve.

Alternative investments often appeal to that mindset. They promise differentiation. They sound advanced. They feel like the next stage of success.

The danger is skipping fundamentals.

No championship team builds its offense entirely around trick plays. Fundamentals win seasons. Advanced strategies work only when layered on top of a strong base.

Alternatives should be additions, not replacements.

Coach's Perspective

A coach would slow you down.

"Know the situation."

"Don't force it."

"Play within the system."

"Value possession."

"Make the simple play."

Real estate and alternatives are situational tools, not default strategies.

Game Situations and Decision Points

Situation one:

You feel pressure to buy because others are buying. Do you evaluate fit or chase validation?

That is choosing discipline over noise.

Situation two:

You are offered a private deal with limited liquidity. Do you assess cash flow needs or focus only on projected returns?

That is reading the slide before dodging.

Situation three:

You want diversification. Do you use REITs or jump into complex structures you do not understand?

That is choosing execution over flash.

Each decision affects your ability to adjust later.

Common Athlete Mistakes and Financial Parallels

Athletes chase highlight plays.

Financially, that leads to risky deals.

Athletes underestimate conditioning.

Financially, that leads to liquidity problems.

Athletes ignore fundamentals.

Financially, that leads to overleveraging.

The patterns repeat.

Winning the Long Game

Real estate and alternative investments can strengthen a financial game plan when used intentionally.

They should add balance, not stress.

They should support flexibility, not remove it.

They should follow fundamentals, not replace them.

You do not need every play in the book.

You need the right plays at the right time.

That is how long seasons are won.

Athlete Takeaways

- Renting and owning are tools, not status symbols
- Real estate requires reps, reserves, and patience
- REITs offer exposure without full-time responsibility
- Alternatives trade liquidity for complexity and risk
- Never force a play that limits future options

Part IV: Managing the Game and Adjustments

Championships are won through smart adjustments.

In lacrosse, the game is rarely decided by the opening whistle. The best teams come out with a plan, but they do not cling to it blindly. They read matchups. They feel momentum shifts. They recognize when a defense changes its look or when legs start to fade. Winning teams adjust without losing their identity. They stay true to their system while making smart, timely corrections.

Managing your investments works the same way.

By this point in the playbook, you have built a foundation. You understand risk. You know how markets work. You have an offense that moves the ball instead of forcing shots. Now the challenge changes. The challenge is not starting. It is managing what you have built without overreacting, overthinking, or abandoning discipline.

This part of the book is about learning how to stay in control as conditions change.

Adjustments Are Not Panic

In lacrosse, an adjustment is not a sign of failure.

If a team switches from man-to-man to zone, you do not panic. You move the ball. You stretch the defense. You attack from a different angle. You trust fundamentals.

Panic adjustments look different.

Panic adjustments are when players freelance. They dodge into traffic. They take rushed shots. They abandon spacing and structure.

In money, panic looks the same.

Selling because markets drop.

Chasing performance because something else is working.

Changing strategy every time headlines get loud.

Smart adjustments are calm. Emotional reactions are chaotic.

Managing Versus Micromanaging

There is a difference between managing the game and overcoaching it.

Good coaches make adjustments between quarters, not after every possession. They let players play. They trust preparation. They intervene when patterns emerge, not when one rep goes wrong.

Managing a portfolio requires the same restraint.

Reviewing matters.

Obsessing does not.

Checking balances daily creates noise. Making changes constantly increases costs and mistakes. The goal is awareness, not control over every bounce.

In lacrosse terms, this is knowing when to call a timeout and when to let the run play out.

Reading the Game as Life Changes

Adjustments are not only about the opponent. They are about your own situation.

In lacrosse, injuries change rotations. Weather changes pace. Fatigue changes matchups. Ignoring those realities leads to breakdowns.

Financially, life does the same thing.

Careers change.

Income shifts.

Families grow.

Goals evolve.

The investment plan that made sense at twenty-two may not fit at thirty-five. Adjusting does not mean starting over. It means realigning the plan with reality.

Good teams adapt to conditions without losing their principles.

Avoiding Over-Adjustment

One of the most common mistakes athletes make is over-adjusting.

One bad possession leads to forcing shots.

One turnover leads to hesitation.

One mistake snowballs into frustration.

Financial over-adjustment follows the same pattern.

Reacting to short-term market moves.

Constantly changing allocations.

Abandoning long-term plans for temporary comfort.

Over-adjustment creates instability. It makes timing worse, not better.

In lacrosse terms, this is changing defensive schemes every possession. Confusion sets in. Communication breaks down. Execution suffers.

Trusting the System Under Pressure

Pressure reveals whether preparation was real.

Late in games, teams do not invent new offenses. They go back to what they trust. They execute the same sets with more focus and urgency.

Money decisions get harder during stress.

Market downturns.

Career uncertainty.

Unexpected expenses.

These moments test discipline. The temptation is to do something just to feel in control. Often, the best move is staying steady and executing the existing plan.

Trusting the system does not mean ignoring information. It means filtering it through experience, goals, and long-term strategy.

Why Adjustments Matter Over Long Seasons

Short seasons reward bursts.

Long seasons reward consistency.

Financial success is a long season.

There will be stretches where nothing seems to work. There will be stretches where everything looks easy. Adjustments keep you balanced through both.

The teams that win championships are rarely the flashiest. They are the ones that protect possession, communicate well, and make smart decisions when conditions change.

That is the mindset this section prepares you for.

What This Part Prepares You To Do

The chapters that follow focus on:

- Balancing different investments like lineups
- Knowing when to buy, hold, or step back
- Making planned changes instead of emotional ones
- Staying composed when pressure rises

This is where maturity shows up.

You are no longer just learning how to play.

You are learning how to manage the game.

And that is where championships are won.

Chapter 15: Asset Allocation and Lineup Balance

Opening Story From the Sport

Every lacrosse coach knows this truth.

You can have the most talented player on the field, but if the lineup around them is wrong, the whole unit struggles. Too many offensive-minded players and the defense breaks down. Too much defense and you cannot generate scoring chances. The best teams are not built around one star. They are built around balance.

Think about a full game rotation.

You need players who can push transition. You need players who settle the ball and protect possession. You need defenders who communicate and recover. You need depth because fatigue shows up late. Lineup balance is not about maximizing one strength. It is about making sure the entire group functions together across four quarters.

Asset allocation is your financial lineup.

It determines how aggressive you are, how resilient you are under pressure, and how well you can adapt when conditions change. You can own great investments and still struggle if the mix is wrong. When the lineup fits, execution feels easier. When it does not, everything feels harder than it should.

The Investing Concept Explained Through Lacrosse

Asset allocation is the way your money is divided among different types of investments, primarily stocks, bonds, and cash.

Financially, this works the same way as lineup construction in lacrosse.

Stocks are your offensive players. They create growth. They push the pace. They score. They also miss shots, go through slumps, and experience volatility. That is part of the job.

Bonds are your defensive core. They slow the game down. They protect leads. They provide stability when things get chaotic. They are not exciting, but they keep you competitive when momentum shifts.

Cash is your possession player. It does not score directly, but it gives you control. Cash allows substitutions, adjustments, and flexibility. It prevents forced decisions when pressure rises.

None of these roles is optional.

A lineup with only scorers gets exposed defensively. A lineup with only defenders never generates offense. A lineup with no depth gets run into the ground. Asset allocation works the same way. Balance creates durability.

Stocks, Bonds, and Cash: Understanding the Roles

Many athletes fall into the same trap financially.

They want to score fast.

Stocks look exciting. Stories circulate about big wins. It feels like the path to quick success. But a portfolio built entirely on stocks is like running all attack with no slide help. It works until it does not.

Bonds get ignored because they are boring. But boring is often the point. Bonds exist to stabilize, not to dominate. They help absorb shocks when markets drop and emotions spike.

Cash often gets dismissed as unproductive. But cash is not wasted space. It is flexibility. It allows you to handle unexpected expenses, take advantage of opportunities, and avoid selling investments at the wrong time.

Good teams respect every role. Good portfolios do the same.

Domestic vs International Exposure: Seeing the Whole Field

Limiting your investments to one country is like only recruiting from one region.

It feels familiar. It feels comfortable. It also increases risk.

Different countries experience different economic cycles, political changes, and growth patterns. While markets are connected, they do not move in perfect sync. International exposure spreads risk across systems instead of concentrating it in one.

In lacrosse terms, this is scouting beyond your conference. You expand your talent pool. You reduce reliance on one style of play. When one matchup is unfavorable, another may work better.

Global diversification does not eliminate losses. It reduces dependence. That distinction matters.

What Diversification Really Means

Diversification is one of the most misunderstood concepts in investing.

It does not mean owning everything.

It does not mean complexity.

It does not mean constant change.

Diversification means spreading risk intelligently so that no single event can derail the entire plan.

In lacrosse terms, diversification is roster depth.

You do not ask one midfielder to carry the offense, defense, and transition for an entire season. You build a roster that can adjust. When one player struggles, another steps up.

Financial concentration increases risk.

Diversification increases resilience.

Career Stage and Lineup Changes

Lineups change over time.

Early in your athletic career, you play faster. You take more risks. You recover quickly. Late-game mistakes matter less because there is time to adjust.

Financially, early career stages often allow for more aggressive allocations. Time is on your side. Volatility is uncomfortable but survivable.

As careers progress, responsibilities grow.

Families.

Mortgages.

Business ownership.

Income variability.

The lineup needs to change. Stability and flexibility matter more. Defense matters more. Cash reserves matter more.

This is not getting conservative. It is getting situationally aware.

The biggest mistake is freezing the lineup. What worked early may fail later. Smart teams adjust rotations as players age. Smart investors adjust allocation as life changes.

Why Asset Allocation Matters More Than Picking Investments

Many athletes obsess over individual investments.

The right stock.

The perfect fund.

The next big opportunity.

In reality, asset allocation drives most long-term outcomes.

A great player in the wrong system struggles.

An average player in the right system thrives.

Asset allocation determines how investments interact under stress. It shapes volatility, behavior, and sustainability. It controls whether you stay disciplined or panic when conditions change.

Picking investments matters.

But lineup balance matters more.

Coach's Perspective: What Would Your Coach Say?

Your coach would not overcomplicate this.

"Do your job."

"Trust the system."

"Play within the lineup."

"Balance wins games."

"Don't beat yourself."

A coach would remind you that forcing shots hurts the team. Ignoring defense costs games late. Overplaying starters leads to breakdowns. The same rules apply financially.

Effort is non-negotiable.

Discipline is expected.

Balance creates consistency.

Game Situations and Decision Points

Situation One: Markets have been strong, and your stock investments are outperforming everything else.

Do you let them dominate the lineup, or do you rebalance to restore balance?

Situation Two: You feel nervous about volatility and want to move everything to cash.

Do you protect possession temporarily, or do you abandon the offense entirely?

Situation Three: Your career changes and income becomes less predictable.

Do you adjust the lineup, or do you pretend nothing changed?

Each decision mirrors a game situation. The right move is rarely extreme. It is usually balanced.

Common Athlete Mistakes and Financial Parallels

Athletes overplay stars.

Financially, that means overconcentration.

Athletes ignore defense.

Financially, that means ignoring stability and risk control.

Athletes resist lineup changes.

Financially, that means outdated allocation.

Talent alone does not win championships. Balance does.

Winning the Long Game

Asset allocation is not about predicting the future. It is about preparing for many versions of it.

Markets will rise and fall.

Careers will change.

Life will throw unexpected challenges.

When the lineup fits, you stay composed. Decisions feel manageable. Discipline holds.

Get the balance right, and everything else works better.

Athlete Takeaways

- Build your lineup, not just your highlight reel
- Offense, defense, and possession all matter
- Balance beats forcing plays
- Adjust your lineup as your career evolves
- Championships are won with disciplined rotations

Chapter 16: Buying, Holding, and Trusting the System

Opening Story From the Sport

Every lacrosse player has experienced this moment.

The ball is moving well. Passes are crisp. Spacing is right. The defense is shifting. Then someone forces a dodge that is not there. Possession is lost. Momentum flips. What was working suddenly unravels.

After the game, the coach does not talk about talent. They talk about discipline.

"You abandoned the system."

"We didn't need a hero play."

"Trust the offense."

Investing works the same way.

Most financial damage does not come from bad intentions. It comes from abandoning a system that was designed to work over time. Buying, holding, and trusting the system is the financial version of running the offense the way it was installed, even when the crowd gets loud and the clock speeds up.

The Investing Concept Explained Through Lacrosse

Investing is not about constant action. It is about controlled execution.

Opening and funding accounts is like learning the playbook. Market orders and limit orders are how you move the ball. Buy-and-hold discipline is trusting the system across the entire game. Avoiding emotional decisions is what separates winning teams from chaotic ones.

Financially, this works the same way as offensive lacrosse.

You do not score by dodging nonstop. You score by moving the ball, creating advantages, and taking high-quality shots when they appear. The system creates opportunities. Panic destroys them.

Opening and Funding Accounts: Getting on the Field

You cannot score if you are not on the field.

Opening investment accounts is not exciting. It feels administrative. But nothing happens until it is done. Retirement accounts, brokerage accounts, and savings vehicles are your entry points into the game.

Many athletes delay this step because it feels overwhelming or unimportant early on. That delay costs time, and time is the most valuable asset you have.

Funding accounts matters just as much as opening them.

An unfunded account is like standing on the sideline in full gear. You look ready, but you are not contributing. Automatic contributions create consistency. They remove hesitation. They keep the ball moving even when motivation drops.

Coaches love reliability. So does investing.

Market Orders vs Limit Orders: Shot Selection Matters

Every shot counts the same on the scoreboard, but not every shot has the same quality.

Market orders mean you buy or sell immediately at the current price.

They are simple and fast. Limit orders allow you to set a specific price and wait for the market to meet it.

In lacrosse terms, this is shot selection.

A market order is taking the open shot when it is there. A limit order is waiting for a cleaner look. Both can be appropriate depending on the situation.

The mistake is overthinking execution.

Many new investors obsess over perfect timing. They wait for the "right moment" and miss entire seasons of progress. In lacrosse, hesitation kills spacing. In investing, hesitation kills compounding.

Execution beats perfection.

Buy-and-Hold Discipline: Trusting the Offense

Buy-and-hold investing is one of the simplest concepts and one of the hardest to follow.

It means you invest according to a plan and allow time, growth, and compounding to do their work. You do not constantly trade. You do not chase every run. You do not abandon the system after one bad quarter.

In lacrosse terms, this is trusting the offense across the entire game.

There will be possessions where nothing opens up. There will be stretches where shots do not fall. That does not mean the offense is broken. It means patience is required.

Buy-and-hold works because markets reward long-term ownership, not short-term reactions. Most returns are generated during relatively short bursts that are impossible to predict. If you are constantly subbing in and out, you miss them.

You do not need to score on every possession.

You need to stay in the game.

Avoiding Emotional Decisions: Crowd Noise and Momentum

Crowd noise affects players.

A bad turnover leads to rushed decisions. A scoring run creates overconfidence. Momentum is powerful, but it is also dangerous.

Financial markets have crowd noise too.

Headlines.

Social media.

Friends.

Fear.

Greed.

Emotional decisions feel urgent. They rarely age well.

Selling during a market drop is like throwing a risky pass while under pressure. It feels like relief in the moment. It often creates bigger problems immediately after.

Buying aggressively during hype is like forcing shots because you feel hot. Sometimes it works. Often it does not.

Discipline is not about ignoring emotion.

It is about not letting emotion run the offense.

Why Doing Less Often Produces More

One of the hardest lessons for athletes is that more action is not always better.

Great offenses are patient.

Great investors are patient.

Constant trading increases mistakes, taxes, fees, and stress. It gives the illusion of control without improving outcomes. The best systems are boring because they work.

In lacrosse, the best possessions often look uneventful until the defense finally breaks. In investing, the best years often feel quiet until you look back and see the progress.

Consistency beats intensity.

Coach's Perspective: What Would Your Coach Say?

Your coach would not sugarcoat this.

"Trust the system."

"Stop forcing plays."

"Value possession."

"Next play."

"Do your job."

A coach knows that emotional decisions spread. One rushed dodge leads to another. One panic sell leads to abandoning the plan entirely.

Effort is expected.

Discipline is demanded.

Execution wins games.

The same applies financially.

Game Situations and Decision Points

Situation One: Markets drop sharply and headlines are negative.

Do you sell to stop the pain, or do you stick to the system and keep possession?

Situation Two: A hot investment is everywhere online.

Do you chase it, or do you stay within your game plan?

Situation Three: Your accounts are set up, but contributions feel tight.

Do you pause entirely, or do you adjust and stay consistent?

Each decision mirrors a lacrosse moment. Panic rarely produces good results.

Common Athlete Mistakes and Financial Parallels

Athletes force hero plays.

Financially, that means chasing hot investments.

Athletes abandon the offense under pressure.

Financially, that means panic selling.

Athletes confuse activity with effectiveness.

Financially, that means overtrading.

Winning teams stay disciplined when it is uncomfortable.

Winning the Long Game

Buying and holding is not passive.

It is disciplined.

Trusting the system does not mean ignoring reality. It means adjusting when necessary without abandoning fundamentals. Markets will move. Life will change. The plan adapts, but the philosophy stays intact.

Possession wins games.

Discipline wins seasons.

Trust wins the long game.

Athlete Takeaways

- Get on the field early and stay involved
- Shot selection matters in investing too
- Trust the system, even when it feels uncomfortable
- Emotion is the fastest way to lose possession
- Long seasons are won by discipline, not hero plays

Chapter 17: Rebalancing and Between-Quarter Adjustments

Opening Story From the Sport

Every lacrosse player has lived through a quarter that did not go as planned.

The offense feels rushed. Slides are late. Matchups are off. You come to the sideline, helmets off, breathing heavy. This is not the moment to panic. It is the moment to adjust.

Good coaches do not scrap the entire game plan between quarters. They identify what drifted. Who is out of position. Where possessions are being lost. Then they make small, intentional adjustments to get the team back in rhythm.

Rebalancing plays that same role in your financial life.

Markets move. Investments perform differently. Over time, your portfolio drifts away from its original setup. Rebalancing is how you bring it back into alignment without emotion, urgency, or panic. It is a between-quarter adjustment, not a rebuild.

The Investing Concept Explained Through Lacrosse

Rebalancing means returning your investments to their intended mix.

If stocks grow faster than bonds, stocks become a larger part of the portfolio. If one asset lags while another surges, the balance changes. Rebalancing trims what has grown and reinforces what has fallen behind.

Financially, this works the same way as lineup adjustments.

If one unit is overplaying minutes because things went well early, fatigue sets in. If another group has been sitting too long, timing gets lost. The coach evens things out so the team can perform over the entire game, not just one stretch.

Rebalancing is not about predicting what comes next.

It is about managing what is already happening.

How Often to Review Investments: Film Study, Not Play-by-Play

You do not review film after every possession.

Constant review creates noise. You overreact to small mistakes. Confidence drops. Decision-making gets sloppy. The same thing happens with investing.

Checking your portfolio daily turns normal volatility into emotional stress. Reviewing too rarely, however, allows drift to go unnoticed.

Most investors benefit from scheduled reviews.

Annual or semiannual check-ins are usually enough. The purpose is awareness, not micromanagement. You are looking for drift, not perfection.

In lacrosse terms, this is film study.

You review tendencies. You notice patterns. You make adjustments before bad habits become costly. You do not replay every missed shot in your head.

Rebalancing Strategies: Managing the Rotation

There are multiple ways to rebalance, just like there are multiple ways to manage minutes.

One approach is calendar-based rebalancing. You adjust on a set schedule, such as once or twice per year, regardless of market conditions. This removes emotion entirely.

Another approach is threshold-based rebalancing. You rebalance only when allocations drift beyond a certain range. This focuses on meaningful changes rather than small fluctuations.

Both approaches work. The key is consistency.

In lacrosse terms, this is rotation management.

You do not overplay one midfielder just because they scored early. You manage minutes so everyone is effective when it matters most. Rebalancing enforces discipline when emotions would otherwise take control.

It often feels counterintuitive.

Rebalancing means trimming what feels good and adding to what feels uncomfortable. That discomfort is not a warning sign. It is usually confirmation that discipline is being applied.

Life Changes and Portfolio Updates: New Opponents, New Game Plans

Not all adjustments are driven by markets.

Life changes matter just as much.

New job.

Marriage.

Children.

Buying a home.

Career shifts.

Health changes.

These events change timelines, cash flow, and risk tolerance. Ignoring them is like running the same defensive scheme against a completely different offense.

Rebalancing handles market drift.

Portfolio updates handle life drift.

Your allocation at 25 should not look the same at 45. Early in your career, growth may take priority. As responsibilities increase, stability and flexibility matter more.

Adaptation is not weakness.

It is situational awareness.

Great players adjust their game as their role changes. Smart investors do the same.

Avoiding Over-Adjustment: When Coaching Hurts Performance

Over-adjustment ruins rhythm.

In sports, constant tinkering creates confusion. Players hesitate. Communication breaks down. Confidence erodes. The same thing happens financially.

Too many changes increase taxes, fees, and mistakes. They also increase stress, which leads to more poor decisions.

Discipline is not inactivity.

It is knowing when action is necessary and when it is not.

Sometimes the best adjustment is staying the course.

In lacrosse terms, this is a coach telling the team, "We're fine. Settle down. Execute."

Most financial damage comes from reacting to short-term noise rather than long-term drift.

Why Rebalancing Protects Behavior, Not Just Numbers

Rebalancing is often described as a mathematical exercise.

It is not.

It is a behavioral tool.

It prevents overconfidence when things are going well.

It prevents panic when things are not.

It keeps decision-making systematic instead of emotional.

Rebalancing forces you to sell high and buy low without trying to time the market. It removes ego from the process. It reinforces the idea that no single asset gets to dominate the game plan forever.

Behavior matters more than precision.

Coach's Perspective: What Would Your Coach Say?

Your coach would be calm and direct.

"Make the adjustment."

"Trust the system."

"Stop chasing."

"Stay composed."

"One possession at a time."

A good coach does not let one quarter define the game. They also do not ignore problems when they appear. Rebalancing lives in that middle ground.

Respond.

Do not react.

Game Situations and Decision Points

Situation One: Stocks have surged and dominate your portfolio.

Do you let momentum run unchecked, or do you rebalance to protect the full season?

Situation Two: Markets are volatile and confidence is low.

Do you abandon the plan, or do you rebalance with discipline?

Situation Three: Your life has changed, but your portfolio has not.

Do you update the game plan, or keep running outdated sets?

Each choice reflects whether you are adjusting with intention or reacting with emotion.

Common Athlete Mistakes and Financial Parallels

Athletes overreact to a bad quarter.

Financially, that means panic selling.

Athletes chase momentum without structure.

Financially, that means letting allocations drift too far.

Athletes resist necessary adjustments.

Financially, that means outdated portfolios.

Championship teams adjust without losing identity.

Winning the Long Game

Rebalancing does not make headlines.

It does not feel exciting.

It works.

Between-quarter adjustments keep teams competitive across the full game. Rebalancing keeps portfolios aligned across full seasons and decades.

You are not trying to win one possession.

You are trying to win the season.

Small, disciplined adjustments protect rhythm, confidence, and long-term outcomes.

Athlete Takeaways

- Review film on a schedule, not after every play
- Adjust the lineup without abandoning the system
- Life changes require game-plan updates
- Over-coaching creates mistakes
- Discipline between quarters wins long games

Chapter 18: The Mental Side of Money

Opening Story From the Sport

Every lacrosse player knows the feeling when momentum shifts.

You are up a goal. The crowd is loud. Possession feels easy. Then a bad turnover happens. A quick goal the other way. Suddenly the sideline tightens. Sticks grip harder. Decisions speed up. The same players with the same skills start making mistakes.

Nothing physical changed.

The mental side took over.

Money works the same way.

Most financial outcomes are not determined by intelligence or information. They are determined by how you handle pressure, confidence, and stress when things are not calm. The mental game of money decides whether good plans get executed or abandoned at the worst possible time.

Pressure, Confidence, and Momentum

Momentum is real in sports.

It is also real in investing.

When markets are rising, confidence increases. People feel smart. Risk feels smaller. Decisions speed up. When markets fall, pressure rises. Fear creeps in. Every decision feels heavy.

Financially, this works the same way as lacrosse momentum.

Confidence can help execution, but it can also create overconfidence. Pressure can sharpen focus, but it can also cause panic. Neither state is inherently bad. The danger comes from letting emotion dictate decisions.

When confidence is high, investors chase returns.

When pressure is high, investors abandon plans.

In lacrosse terms, this is forcing dodges when you should move the ball or rushing shots when you should reset the offense.

The goal is not to eliminate emotion.

The goal is to prevent emotion from calling the plays.

Crowd Noise and Comparison

Crowds matter.

In lacrosse, home-field energy can lift you. It can also distract you. Players feel the urge to make something happen instead of making the right play.

Financial markets have crowd noise too.

Headlines.

Social media.

Friends.

Co-workers.

Online forums.

Everyone has an opinion when markets move. When things are going well, the noise encourages risk. When things are going poorly, the noise amplifies fear.

Comparison is the most dangerous part.

You see someone else's success. A hot stock. A big return. A lifestyle upgrade. Suddenly your own plan feels slow, boring, or wrong.

In lacrosse terms, this is leaving your assignment because you see someone else making a play.

Crowd noise makes you forget your role.

Comparison makes you abandon your system.

Herd behavior feels safe because everyone is doing it.

It rarely produces good outcomes.

Why Discipline Breaks Under Stress

Discipline is easy when things are calm.

The real test comes under stress.

Markets drop.

Income fluctuates.

Life changes.

Unexpected expenses appear.

Without systems, discipline becomes willpower.

Willpower always loses.

Former athletes understand this better than most. In sports, discipline is built into the environment. Practice times. Lift schedules. Film sessions. Accountability is external.

Money does not come with a coach or a whistle.

If you rely on motivation, confidence, or feelings, discipline breaks when pressure rises. That is why so many smart people make poor financial decisions at the worst moments.

Building Systems for Discipline

Discipline is not a personality trait.

It is a system.

The most successful investors build guardrails that protect them from themselves.

Automatic contributions.

Diversified portfolios.

Scheduled reviews.

Rebalancing rules.

Clear criteria for decisions.

These systems do the thinking when emotions are loud.

In lacrosse terms, this is running a practiced offense under pressure. You do not improvise every possession. You trust spacing, timing, and reps.

Systems slow the game down.

They remove urgency.

They remove ego.

They remove reaction.

You are not trying to be perfect.

You are trying to be consistent.

Consistency wins more games than brilliance.

Staying Composed in Rough Water

Volatility is normal.

Markets move up and down.

Returns come unevenly.

Progress feels invisible for long stretches.

The biggest mistake investors make is treating volatility as danger instead of as part of the game.

In lacrosse terms, this is panicking every time the opponent scores.

Great teams respond.

They do not react.

Staying composed means:

Limiting how often you check results.

Remembering why the plan exists.

Focusing on controllables.

Avoiding big changes during emotional moments.

The best financial decisions are often boring.

The worst ones usually feel urgent.

If something feels like it requires immediate action, that is usually a sign to pause.

Confidence Without Arrogance

Confidence matters.

You need confidence to stay invested.

You need confidence to trust long-term plans.

You need confidence to ignore noise.

But confidence without humility becomes arrogance.

Arrogance shows up as:

Believing you can time the market.

Believing you are smarter than everyone else.

Believing risk no longer applies.

In lacrosse terms, this is hero ball.

Confidence should come from preparation and systems, not from recent success. When confidence is grounded, it survives setbacks. When it is built on outcomes, it collapses under pressure.

Coach's Perspective: What Would Your Coach Say?

Your coach would be blunt.

"Control what you can control."

"Next possession."

"Stay locked in."

"Don't beat yourself."

"Trust the work."

They would not let emotion run the game.

They would not let the crowd dictate decisions.

They would demand composure when things get uncomfortable.

Mental toughness is not about intensity.

It is about discipline under pressure.

Game Situations and Decision Points

Situation One: Markets drop sharply and headlines are negative.

Do you abandon the plan or stick to your system?

Situation Two: Markets surge and everyone is talking about quick wins.

Do you chase momentum or rebalance with discipline?

Situation Three: You feel restless and want to "do something."

Do you act emotionally or trust the structure you built?

Each situation tests the mental side of money more than the technical side.

Common Athlete Mistakes and Financial Parallels

Athletes play to the crowd.

Financially, that leads to comparison and herd behavior.

Athletes force plays under pressure.

Financially, that leads to panic selling or chasing returns.

Athletes abandon the system when confidence spikes.

Financially, that leads to overconfidence and unnecessary risk.

The same habits that cost games also cost financial results.

Winning the Long Game

The mental side of money determines whether good plans survive real-world stress.

You do not need perfect decisions.

You need repeatable discipline.

Markets will test patience.

Life will test confidence.

Noise will test focus.

Athletes who succeed financially treat money like competition.

They stay composed.

They trust preparation.

They execute under pressure.

The scoreboard will move.

Your job is to stay in the game.

Athlete Takeaways

- Pressure exposes habits, not intelligence
- Crowd noise leads to mistakes if you chase it
- Systems protect discipline when emotions spike
- Confidence must be grounded in preparation, not results
- Staying composed under stress wins long seasons

Part V: The Full Season and Life After Lacrosse

The game does not end when the final whistle blows. It changes.

A lacrosse season is not defined by one game.

It is defined by practices no one sees, midweek film sessions, bus rides, injuries, adjustments, wins that feel routine, and losses that linger. The best teams understand this early. They do not treat the season as a series of highlights. They treat it as a long grind that requires patience, adaptability, and perspective.

Life after lacrosse works the same way.

The structure that once defined your days disappears. The feedback loop changes. The scoreboard fades. But the season continues. Just without uniforms, officials, or a clearly marked field.

This part of the book is about navigating that full season.

The End of the Schedule Does Not Mean the End of the Game

In lacrosse, your calendar is set.

Practice times. Lift sessions. Film. Games. Travel. Recovery. Everything is planned. Discipline is enforced externally. You show up, or there are consequences.

After lacrosse, the schedule vanishes.

No one tells you when to train.

No one tracks your reps.

No one checks your preparation.

This feels like freedom at first. For many former athletes, it quietly becomes drift.

Financially, this is where habits break.

Saving becomes optional.

Planning gets delayed.

Goals become vague.

Nothing goes wrong immediately, which makes the problem harder to see.

In lacrosse terms, this is a long season without a coach setting the lineup. If you do not build structure yourself, performance declines without warning.

Why the "Full Season" Mindset Matters Financially

Most people approach money in short bursts.

A raise.

A bonus.

A big purchase.

A market swing.

Athletes think differently.

You are trained to think in seasons. You understand that conditioning matters more than one sprint. You understand that consistency beats intensity. You understand that recovery, discipline, and patience win over time.

The mistake former athletes make is abandoning that mindset once competition ends.

Money rewards season-long thinking.

Career growth happens over years, not months.

Investments compound slowly, then suddenly.

Good decisions rarely feel exciting in the moment.

If you expect immediate results, frustration sets in.

If you commit to the long season, progress becomes predictable.

Identity After Lacrosse

One of the hardest adjustments after sports is identity.

For years, you were a lacrosse player.

That label came with respect, community, and clarity.

When it ends, many athletes feel unanchored.

Financially, this shows up as:

Chasing status.

Overspending to feel successful.

Making decisions to prove something instead of to build something.

In lacrosse terms, this is playing for highlights instead of possession.

Life after lacrosse requires a new identity, not a replacement trophy.

You are not "former."

You are evolving.

The discipline, toughness, and awareness you built on the field still apply. The scoreboard just looks different now.

Replacing Competition With Purpose

Competition does not disappear.

It changes form.

Some athletes replace competition with income.

Others replace it with titles.

Others replace it with lifestyle markers.

Those substitutes rarely satisfy for long.

Purpose lasts longer than competition.

Purpose can be:

Building a career.

Supporting a family.

Mentoring others.

Creating flexibility.

Gaining control over your time.

Money is a tool for purpose, not a score.

In lacrosse terms, this is understanding that winning possession matters more than taking low-quality shots. Purpose gives direction to effort. Without it, energy gets wasted.

The Long Season Requires Adjustments

No season goes exactly as planned.

Injuries happen.

Roles change.

Opponents adjust.

Conditions shift.

Financial life is no different.

Careers change.

Markets move.

Families grow.

Priorities evolve.

Former athletes struggle when they expect linear progress. The ability to adjust without panicking is what separates sustainable success from burnout.

Adjustments are not failure.

They are professionalism.

The best teams stay composed, make smart changes, and protect the long view.

Coach's Perspective: What Would Your Coach Say?

Your coach would remind you:

"This is a long season."

"Stay disciplined."

"Control what you can control."

"Do not drift."

"Finish strong."

They would not let one bad stretch define you.

They would not let early success make you careless.

They would demand consistency when no one is watching.

Winning the Long Game

Life after lacrosse is not about replacing what you lost.

It is about applying what you learned.

Discipline.

Structure.

Preparation.

Patience.

Teamwork.

When you approach money and life like a full season, not a single game, outcomes improve dramatically.

The game continues.

You are still in it.

You just play it differently now.

The athletes who win long after lacrosse are not the ones chasing moments.

They are the ones who commit to the season.

Chapter 19: Taxes and Where You Keep Possession

In lacrosse, possession is everything.

You can have elite shooters, great sets, and a solid game plan, but if you keep turning the ball over, none of it matters. The teams that win consistently are the teams that value possession. They protect the ball, move it with purpose, and understand where on the field they want to attack from.

Taxes work the same way.

You can earn a great income. You can invest well. You can make smart decisions. But if you ignore taxes, you are giving away possession on every clear. Where you hold your money and how it is taxed matters just as much as how much you make.

This chapter is about learning how to keep possession financially.

Opening Story From the Sport

Every lacrosse player has lived this.

Your team is dominating the stat sheet. More shots. More ground balls. Better looks. But the scoreboard is tight because turnovers keep killing momentum. A forced dodge here. A rushed pass there. Each mistake hands the ball right back to the other team.

The coach is furious, not because the talent is lacking, but because the fundamentals are being ignored.

"Protect the ball," they keep saying.

"Value possession."

"Stop beating yourselves."

Financially, taxes are one of the biggest ways athletes beat themselves without realizing it.

Taxable vs Tax-Advantaged Accounts

In lacrosse, not all field positions are equal.

Where you attack from matters. A clean look from the middle is different than a low-angle shot on the run. Same effort. Very different results.

Taxable accounts are like playing offense anywhere on the field. You can move freely. You can access the ball anytime. But every move comes with friction. Interest, dividends, and gains are taxed as they occur.

Tax-advantaged accounts are like setting up your offense in the sweet spots. They come with rules, but the efficiency is higher.

Retirement accounts, health savings accounts, and similar structures allow your money to grow with fewer turnovers to taxes along the way.

Financially, this works the same way as offensive spacing. You want to take your best opportunities from the most efficient spots on the field.

Using only taxable accounts is not wrong. Ignoring tax-advantaged accounts is inefficient.

Tax-Deferred vs Tax-Free Growth

This is where many athletes get confused.

Tax-deferred growth means you delay paying taxes until later. You may get a benefit now, but withdrawals are taxed in the future.

Tax-free growth means you pay taxes upfront and avoid them later, assuming you follow the rules.

Neither option is automatically better.

In lacrosse terms, this is choosing between dodging early or moving the ball and attacking later. Both can work. Timing matters. Situation matters.

The mistake is assuming one approach fits every possession.

If you are early in your career and expect income to rise, tax-free growth can be powerful. If income is high now and expected to be lower later, tax deferral may make sense.

Good teams understand clock management. Good financial plans understand tax timing.

Asset Location Basics

Asset allocation is about what you own.

Asset location is about where you keep it.

Some investments generate more taxable income. Others are more tax-efficient. Putting the wrong assets in the wrong accounts quietly costs you possession year after year.

In lacrosse terms, this is poor spacing.

You do not crowd your best dodgers into the same area. You do not leave shooters standing where they cannot be effective. Where players line up affects execution without changing talent.

Financially, asset location improves results without increasing risk. It is one of the most overlooked fundamentals because it is not exciting. It just works.

Common Tax Mistakes Athletes Make

The same mistakes show up repeatedly.

Ignoring taxes entirely until filing season.

Using only one type of account because it feels simpler.

Making decisions based on headlines instead of personal context.

Letting income increases go untaxed without planning.

Assuming taxes are someone else's problem.

In lacrosse terms, this is freelancing on offense without understanding the set. It feels fast. It looks aggressive. It usually leads to turnovers.

Taxes reward preparation, not reaction.

Coach's Perspective: What Would Your Coach Say?

Your coach would be blunt.

"Value the ball."

"Stop forcing it."

"Play smart, not just fast."

"Every possession matters."

"Don't beat yourself."

They would not accept sloppy fundamentals just because the opponent looks beatable. They would demand discipline even when you feel comfortable.

Taxes are part of the game whether you like it or not. Ignoring them is not toughness. It is carelessness.

Game Situations and Decision Points

You earn more money this year.

Do you adjust where you save, or do you let taxes take a bigger bite?

You start investing.

Do you think about tax impact, or do you focus only on returns?

You wait until April to think about taxes.

Do you plan ahead next season, or repeat the scramble?

Each decision either protects possession or hands it away.

Common Athlete Mistakes and Financial Parallels

Athletes force shots.

Financially, that means ignoring tax efficiency.

Athletes ignore spacing.

Financially, that means poor asset location.

Athletes react late.

Financially, that means missed planning opportunities.

The scoreboard does not care how hard you worked. It reflects execution.

Winning the Long Game

You cannot eliminate taxes.

You can manage them.

Teams that value possession do not rush. They move the ball. They wait for good looks. Over time, efficiency wins.

Financial success works the same way. Smart tax decisions compound quietly. The benefit does not always feel dramatic in the moment. It shows up years later in flexibility, options, and control.

Keeping possession is not flashy. It is how games are won.

Athlete Takeaways

- Value possession. Taxes are part of the game.
- Where you keep your money matters as much as how much you earn.
- Timing beats force. Tax-deferred and tax-free both have roles.
- Good spacing improves efficiency without extra effort.
- Protect possession and the scoreboard takes care of itself.

Chapter 20: Retirement Accounts and Financial Independence

In lacrosse, nobody trains only for the first quarter.

Conditioning is built for the full game. Smart teams think about possessions late in the fourth, not just highlights early. You pace yourself, manage energy, and make decisions with the end in mind. Players who burn out early do not matter when the game is on the line.

Retirement planning works the same way.

Financial independence is not about a specific age. It is about control. It is the ability to decide how, when, and why you work without being forced by money. Retirement accounts are the long-game tools designed to help you maintain possession all the way to the final whistle.

This chapter is about understanding those tools and using them with intention.

Opening Story From the Sport

Every lacrosse player knows the difference between being in shape and being *game-fit*.

You can look strong in warmups and still fade late. You can dominate early possessions and still lose because your legs are gone when it matters. Coaches condition for the end of the game because that is where discipline shows up.

Retirement accounts exist for the same reason.

They are not designed for excitement. They are designed for endurance. They reward players who commit early, stay consistent, and respect the rules of the game.

Employer Plans and Pensions

For many athletes and former athletes, an employer-sponsored retirement plan is the first real entry point into long-term investing.

401(k)s, 403(b)s, and similar plans allow you to contribute directly from your paycheck. That matters because it removes friction. The money moves before you can spend it. Discipline is built into the system.

Employer matches are especially important.

In lacrosse terms, an employer match is a man-up opportunity. You do not overthink it. You take it. Ignoring a match is like refusing an open look because you want a better highlight later.

Some careers still include pensions. These are structured income promises in retirement, often based on years of service. They are less common now, but when available, they play an important defensive role in long-term planning.

The key is understanding what your employer offers and using it fully. These benefits are part of your compensation, whether you value them or not.

Traditional and Roth IRAs

IRAs give you flexibility beyond employer plans.

A Traditional IRA allows money to grow tax-deferred. A Roth IRA allows money to grow tax-free if rules are followed. Both have contribution limits and eligibility rules that matter.

In lacrosse terms, these are different offensive options.

A Traditional IRA is like slowing the game down now to preserve energy later. A Roth IRA is like pushing early so the finish is cleaner. Neither is automatically better. The right choice depends on income, tax rates, and long-term expectations.

Many athletes benefit from using both over time. Balance creates options. Options create control.

The mistake is waiting because the rules feel confusing. Clarity comes from participation, not avoidance.

Contribution and Withdrawal Rules

Retirement accounts come with rules for a reason.

Contribution limits exist to encourage steady progress instead of last-minute panic. Withdrawal restrictions exist to protect long-term discipline. Penalties exist to prevent players from abandoning the plan when emotions spike.

In lacrosse terms, this is the shot clock and substitution box.

Structure keeps the game fair. It forces decision-making within boundaries. You can still play creatively, but you cannot ignore the rules and expect success.

Understanding the rules does not restrict you. It keeps you from committing unnecessary fouls that cost you later.

Retirement Income Basics

Saving for retirement is only half the game.

Using that money intelligently matters just as much.

Retirement income planning focuses on how money is withdrawn, how taxes are managed, and how long assets need to last. This is not about maximizing one year. It is about sustaining decades.

In lacrosse terms, this is fourth-quarter possession.

You protect the ball. You choose shots carefully. You manage the clock. You do not rush just because the goal is close.

Athletes who ignore this phase often overspend early and struggle later. Those who plan finish strong.

Why Athletes Struggle With Retirement Planning

Athletes are trained to live in the present.

Next practice. Next game. Next season. Retirement feels abstract, distant, and optional. That mindset works on the field. Financially, it creates problems.

Money rewards early action because of compounding. Waiting does not just delay progress. It permanently reduces what is possible.

In lacrosse terms, skipping conditioning does not just hurt one game. It affects the entire season.

You do not need to start big.

You do need to start.

Coach's Perspective: What Would Your Coach Say?

Your coach would not overcomplicate this.

"Take the free reps."

"Play the long game."

"Don't quit on the system."

"Conditioning wins late."

"Finish strong."

They would not care how far away the championship feels. They would care that you showed up today.

Retirement planning is not about predicting the future. It is about preparing for it.

Game Situations and Decision Points

Your employer offers a match.

Do you take it immediately or leave it on the table?

You qualify for an IRA.

Do you open it now or tell yourself you will later?

You want flexibility.

Do you build structure now or hope options appear later?

The choices you make early determine how much control you have later.

Common Athlete Mistakes and Financial Parallels

Athletes skip conditioning.

Financially, that means delaying retirement savings.

Athletes focus only on scoring.

Financially, that means ignoring income planning.

Athletes underestimate endurance.

Financially, that means running out of money too soon.

The game always lasts longer than you think.

Winning the Long Game

Financial independence is built the same way championships are built.

Quiet work.

Consistent reps.

Respect for fundamentals.

Patience when results are not immediate.

Retirement accounts are not exciting. They are powerful. They protect your future self the same way conditioning protects your late-game performance.

Start early. Stay consistent. Trust the system.

Athlete Takeaways

- Retirement accounts are conditioning for the fourth quarter of life
- Employer matches are man-up opportunities you do not skip
- Traditional and Roth accounts are different offensive tools, not rivals
- Rules protect discipline and long-term control
- Financial independence comes from preparation, not timing

Chapter 21: Housing and Major Financial Decisions

In lacrosse, not every possession is a fast break.

Some situations call for patience. You slow the ball down. You survey the field. You wait for the defense to shift before you attack. Great players understand that forcing a play just because the opportunity *feels* big often leads to turnovers.

Housing and major financial decisions work the same way.

Buying a home. Financing a car. Signing a long-term lease. Taking on debt that will shape your cash flow for years. These are not routine possessions. They are momentum-shifting moments. If you rush them, you can spend years trying to recover possession.

This chapter is about slowing the game down when the stakes are high.

Opening Story From the Sport

Every lacrosse player has seen this mistake.

Late in a tight game, a midfielder dodges into traffic with no outlet. The crowd gets loud. The moment feels big. Instead of moving the ball and resetting, they force a shot that had no chance. Turnover. Fast break the other way. Momentum gone.

After the game, the coach does not talk about effort.

They talk about decision-making.

"You didn't need to score right there."

"You needed to protect possession."

"Big moments require patience."

Housing and large purchases demand that same discipline.

Renting vs Buying: Tools, Not Identities

Renting and buying are not statements about success.

They are tools.

Renting provides flexibility. Lower upfront costs. Easier exits. Fewer surprises. It allows you to move for opportunities, adapt to income changes, and preserve cash.

Buying provides stability. Potential appreciation. Forced savings through mortgage payments. A sense of permanence. It can make sense when income is steady and timelines are long.

In lacrosse terms, renting is keeping the ball moving. Buying is setting up in a settled offense. Neither is better in every situation.

The mistake athletes make is treating buying a home like scoring a goal instead of managing possession. They buy because it feels like progress, because peers are doing it, or because it signals adulthood.

That mindset leads to rushed decisions.

The right question is not "Can I buy?"

It is "Does buying fit my current game plan?"

Mortgages and Down Payments

A mortgage is long-term debt tied to a physical asset.

That alone makes it different from most other purchases.

The monthly payment matters, but it is not the full cost. Property taxes. Insurance. Maintenance. Repairs. Time. Stress. These responsibilities exist whether you feel ready or not.

In lacrosse terms, this is committing to heavy minutes.

If you are in great shape, heavy minutes are manageable. If conditioning is questionable or your role is unstable, those minutes catch up to you fast.

Down payments affect pressure.

A larger down payment can lower monthly stress and reduce risk. A smaller down payment preserves cash and flexibility but increases leverage. Neither choice is inherently right or wrong. The right answer depends on income stability, emergency savings, and how much margin for error you have.

What matters most is not stretching to the maximum loan you qualify for. That is like staying on the field even when you are gassed because you *can*, not because you *should*.

Cars, Leases, and Financing Traps

Cars are one of the most common financial turnovers athletes make.

They are emotional purchases.

They are easy to finance.

They depreciate.

They rarely improve long-term outcomes.

Monthly payments hide the real cost. Long loan terms make expensive cars feel affordable. Leases lower payments but limit flexibility. Interest quietly compounds against you.

In lacrosse terms, this is forcing a low-angle shot early in the clock because it looks open. It feels aggressive. Over time, it kills efficiency.

Transportation is a tool.

It should get you to practice, work, and life reliably. It should not dominate your cash flow or dictate your future decisions.

Athletes often justify expensive cars as rewards for hard work. The problem is that the reward keeps charging interest long after the excitement fades.

Planning Large Purchases

Big purchases deserve planning.

That means understanding:

- Total cost, not just monthly payment
- Impact on cash flow
- Effect on savings and investing
- Loss of flexibility
- Worst-case scenarios

If a purchase forces you to pause retirement contributions, drain emergency savings, or rely on future income increases, it is too aggressive.

In lacrosse terms, this is clock awareness.

You do not take a risky shot when protecting a lead. You do not force action when patience wins the game. You make the simple play.

Big financial decisions should make your life easier, not tighter.

Why Athletes Feel Pressure Around These Decisions

Athletes are competitive by nature.

They compare progress.

They track milestones.

They notice what teammates and peers are doing.

That makes housing and cars especially dangerous. They are visible. They feel like scoreboards in a world where metrics are less clear.

Buying a home can feel like winning.

Driving a nice car can feel like success.

But feelings are not fundamentals.

The goal is not to look ahead. The goal is to stay in control.

Coach's Perspective: What Would Your Coach Say?

Your coach would slow you down.

"Check the situation."

"Know the clock."

"Protect possession."

"Make the simple play."

"Don't force it."

They would not care how good the opportunity looks if it compromises the team later.

Big decisions deserve patience. Emotion has no place in execution.

Game Situations and Decision Points

You feel pressure to buy a home.

Do you evaluate fit, or do you chase validation?

You qualify for financing.

Do you ask if you *should* take it, or just if you *can*?

You want a nicer car.

Do you consider long-term impact, or just the payment?

These moments do not come often. Their consequences last.

Common Athlete Mistakes and Financial Parallels

Athletes rush big moments.

Financially, that leads to overcommitment.

Athletes focus on highlights.

Financially, that leads to expensive purchases.

Athletes underestimate recovery time.

Financially, that leads to stress and regret.

The scoreboard always reflects discipline, not excitement.

Winning the Long Game

Housing and major purchases should support your life, not restrict it.

Flexibility matters.

Cash flow matters.

Peace of mind matters.

The smartest financial decisions are often the ones no one applauds. They keep options open. They protect possession. They allow you to adapt when life changes.

You do not need to win every possession.

You do need to avoid costly turnovers.

Athlete Takeaways

- Renting and buying are tools, not scoreboards
- Mortgages require stability, margin, and planning
- Cars should support life, not signal success
- Monthly payments hide long-term consequences
- Big decisions demand patience, not pressure

Chapter 22: Your Career Is Your Long Stick

In lacrosse, the long stick changes everything.

It extends your reach. It gives you leverage. It allows you to disrupt plays, win ground balls, and influence the game even when you are not touching the ball every possession. When used correctly, it makes the entire defense better. When neglected or misused, it becomes a liability.

Your career plays that same role in your financial life.

Investments matter. Budgeting matters. Protection matters. But nothing drives long-term financial outcomes more than your ability to earn, grow, adapt, and stay relevant over time. Treating your career casually is like ignoring the fundamentals of using your long stick and hoping the rest of the team carries you.

This chapter is about understanding your career as your most powerful financial tool and learning how to use it with intention.

Opening Story From the Sport

Every lacrosse player knows this difference.

Two defenders have similar athleticism. One understands angles, positioning, and how to use the long stick to control space. The other just reacts. One dictates the play. The other is always late.

The difference is not effort. It is awareness and development.

Careers work the same way.

Two people can work equally hard. One steadily increases income, flexibility, and opportunity. The other feels stuck despite effort. The difference is not talent. It is how intentionally the career is managed.

Salary vs Total Compensation

Salary is the most obvious number on the offer letter.

It is also the most misleading.

Total compensation includes:

- Bonuses and incentives
- Employer retirement contributions
- Health insurance and other benefits
- Time off and flexibility
- Professional development opportunities
- Vesting schedules and long-term incentives

Two jobs with the same salary can produce very different financial outcomes depending on these factors.

In lacrosse terms, salary is caused turnovers or goals scored. Total compensation is ground balls, minutes played, matchup assignments, and trust from the coaching staff. You cannot evaluate impact from one stat.

Athletes often chase salary because it feels measurable. But higher salary with poor benefits, limited growth, or burnout risk can be a net loss over time.

Smart players look at the whole field before committing.

Job Changes and Benefits

Changing jobs is like changing teams.

New system.

New expectations.

New culture.

New benefits.

Every move resets certain variables that directly affect your finances. Health insurance changes. Retirement plans change. Vesting schedules restart. Time-off policies differ. These details matter far more than most people realize.

In lacrosse terms, this is learning a new defensive scheme. You cannot assume it works like the old one. If you do, mistakes happen fast.

Athletes sometimes underestimate this transition because they focus on the role or title instead of the system. That leads to surprises that show up as higher costs, lost benefits, or stalled progress.

Job changes can accelerate growth when planned intentionally. Poorly timed or emotionally driven moves often create instability that spills into every other financial decision.

Negotiation Basics

Negotiation is not confrontation.

It is communication.

Many athletes hesitate to negotiate because it feels uncomfortable. That is ironic. You have competed for roster spots, minutes, and roles your entire life. Negotiation uses the same skills.

Preparation.

Awareness.

Timing.

Confidence.

In lacrosse terms, negotiation is positioning.

You do not demand the ball without earning trust. You show value through performance. You understand leverage. You communicate clearly.

Negotiation is not about squeezing every dollar out of an employer. It is about aligning expectations and making sure value is recognized.

Small improvements early in a career compound dramatically over time. A modest salary increase affects bonuses, raises, retirement contributions, and confidence. Avoiding negotiation does not preserve harmony. It often leaves opportunity on the table.

Side Income and Entrepreneurship

Side income can be a powerful tool.

Coaching.

Consulting.

Content creation.

Business ownership.

Speaking.

Training.

These opportunities can increase flexibility, diversify income, and build new skills. They can also introduce complexity, taxes, risk, and distraction.

In lacrosse terms, this is adding another dimension to your game.

A defender who can push transition offense becomes harder to game plan against. A player who tries to do everything without structure creates chaos.

Side income should support your main career, not sabotage it. The mistake athletes make is chasing quick money without considering time, energy, and opportunity cost.

Just because you *can* take on extra work does not mean you *should*.

Why Athletes Struggle With Career Management

Athletes are conditioned to focus on performance, not politics.

You expect effort to be visible.

You expect merit to be rewarded.

You expect clarity from leadership.

The workplace does not always work that way.

Career growth often depends on communication, visibility, relationships, and timing. Athletes who wait quietly for recognition often feel overlooked. Those who advocate professionally tend to grow faster.

This does not mean compromising values. It means understanding the environment you are playing in.

Ignoring the system does not make it fairer. It makes it harder.

Career Risk Is Financial Risk

Your income funds everything.

Savings.

Investing.

Housing.

Insurance.

Flexibility.

Career instability increases financial stress even if spending habits are reasonable. That is why career planning is financial planning.

In lacrosse terms, this is controlling possession on defense. When you protect the ball, everything else works. When you lose it, the entire team scrambles.

Developing skills, maintaining relationships, and staying adaptable protects your financial foundation.

Coach's Perspective: What Would Your Coach Say?

Your coach would be direct.

"Develop your stick."

"Know your role."

"Earn trust."

"Communicate."

"Don't waste reps."

They would not accept raw talent without development. They would not excuse poor preparation. They would expect you to take ownership of your growth.

Careers are built, not discovered.

Game Situations and Decision Points

You receive a job offer.

Do you evaluate total compensation or focus only on salary?

You feel underpaid.

Do you prepare and negotiate, or stay silent and frustrated?

You consider side income.

Do you plan for impact and risk, or chase quick money?

Each choice compounds.

Common Athlete Mistakes and Financial Parallels

Athletes rely on talent alone.

Financially, that means neglecting development.

Athletes avoid uncomfortable conversations.

Financially, that leaves money and opportunity on the table.

Athletes overextend.

Financially, that leads to burnout and instability.

Effort without strategy is wasted energy.

Winning the Long Game

Your career is your longest race.

It requires pacing.

Adaptation.

Skill development.

Intentional decisions.

When your career is developed and protected, everything else works better. Investing becomes easier. Planning feels calmer. Options expand.

Treat your career like the long stick it is. Use it with purpose. Maintain it. Develop it.

That leverage compounds for decades.

Athlete Takeaways

- Your career is your biggest financial advantage
- Total compensation matters more than salary alone
- Job changes reset systems and benefits
- Negotiation is positioning, not confrontation
- Side income should strengthen, not distract from, your main game

Chapter 23: Estate Planning Basics Everyone Needs

In lacrosse, the best teams never wait until the final possession to decide who takes the shot.

Roles are defined long before the game is on the line. Everyone knows who clears, who quarterbacks the offense, who slides first, and who covers the crease. When pressure hits, decisions are automatic. Confusion is eliminated because preparation already happened.

Estate planning works the same way.

It is not about expecting something bad to happen. It is about making sure that if something *does* happen, the right people are in place, decisions are clear, and nothing is left to chance. Estate planning is not about death. It is about control, clarity, and protecting the people you care about.

Athletes who delay this conversation usually do so for the same reason teams avoid uncomfortable drills. It feels unnecessary until it is not. By then, it is too late.

Opening Story From the Sport

Every lacrosse player has experienced this nightmare.

A broken play. Two defenders slide at the same time. No one covers the crease. The offense scores an easy goal, not because of talent, but because of confusion. Afterward, the coach is furious.

"You didn't talk."

"You didn't know your role."

"You left it up to chance."

Estate planning failures look exactly like that. Assets end up in the wrong hands. Decisions get delayed. Families argue. Courts get involved. All because no one took the time to define roles ahead of time.

Why Estate Planning Matters Earlier Than You Think

Most athletes think estate planning is something for later.

Later in life.

Later in your career.

Later when you have "enough" money.

That mindset causes more damage than almost any other financial delay.

Estate planning is not about how much you have. It is about who makes decisions if you cannot and who receives what you leave behind. If you have a bank account, a retirement account, insurance, or people who depend on you, estate planning already applies.

In lacrosse terms, this is like waiting until playoffs to install defensive slides. You do not prepare for pressure under pressure. You prepare long before it arrives.

Wills and Trusts

A will is the most basic estate planning document.

It outlines:

- Who receives your assets
- Who handles your affairs
- Who becomes guardian for minor children, if applicable

Without a will, the state decides. That process is slow, expensive, public, and impersonal. It does not care about your preferences, relationships, or intentions.

In lacrosse terms, no will means no game plan. The officials take over, and you lose control of execution.

A trust is a more advanced tool.

Trusts can:

- Avoid probate
- Provide privacy
- Control timing of distributions
- Protect beneficiaries from poor decisions or outside risks
- Simplify administration

Trusts are not just for wealthy families. They are for people who want structure and clarity. Just like advanced offensive sets are not only for elite teams, trusts are not only for ultra-high-net-worth households.

A will is better than nothing. A trust is better than confusion.

Beneficiaries and Account Titling

This is one of the most misunderstood parts of estate planning.

Many assets do not pass through a will at all.

Retirement accounts.

Life insurance policies.

Certain bank and brokerage accounts.

These assets pass by beneficiary designation.

If beneficiary forms are outdated, incorrect, or missing, your intentions may not matter. A will does not override a beneficiary designation. This is where many families get blindsided.

Account titling also matters.

Joint ownership.

Individual ownership.

Trust ownership.

Each has different implications for access, taxes, and control.

In lacrosse terms, this is lineup clarity.

If two players think they are sliding first, no one actually does. If no one knows who is covering the crease, the ball ends up in the net. Estate planning failures often come from miscommunication, not bad intentions.

Beneficiary reviews are simple. Ignoring them is costly.

Powers of Attorney

A power of attorney allows someone to act on your behalf if you cannot.

There are two primary types:

- Financial power of attorney
- Healthcare power of attorney

A financial power of attorney allows someone to manage money, pay bills, handle accounts, and make financial decisions if you are incapacitated.

A healthcare power of attorney allows someone to make medical decisions if you are unable to communicate.

Without these documents, loved ones may be unable to help you when you need it most. Banks freeze accounts. Medical decisions get delayed. Stress and frustration escalate.

In lacrosse terms, this is not having a backup long stick defender. If someone goes down, the system still needs to function. Powers of attorney keep the game running when you cannot be on the field.

Healthcare Directives

Healthcare directives outline your medical wishes.

They guide doctors and loved ones during serious situations. They reduce guesswork. They remove emotional burden from family members who might otherwise be forced to decide under pressure.

These conversations are uncomfortable. Avoiding them does not protect anyone. It simply shifts the burden onto the people you care about.

In lacrosse terms, this is film review for worst-case scenarios.

You do not review film because you expect to fail. You review film so mistakes do not repeat. Healthcare directives do the same thing. They create clarity before emotion takes over.

Why Athletes Avoid Estate Planning

Athletes avoid estate planning for predictable reasons.

It feels morbid.

It feels unnecessary.

It feels like admitting vulnerability.

Sports culture rewards toughness and forward focus. Estate planning feels like the opposite. In reality, it is responsibility, not pessimism.

You plan rides and clears even when you expect to dominate.

You plan substitutions even when you expect to stay healthy.

Estate planning is no different.

Ignoring it does not make you tougher. It makes your family's life harder.

Coach's Perspective: What Would Your Coach Say?

Your coach would not sugarcoat this.

"Handle your business."

"Do your job."

"Protect the team."

"Don't leave it to chance."

"Preparation is respect."

They would not accept excuses when fundamentals are ignored. Estate planning is a fundamental.

It is not about fear.

It is about responsibility.

Game Situations and Decision Points

You assume you are too young.

Do you delay, or do you take control?

Your life changes. Marriage. Kids. Assets.

Do you update documents or ignore reality?

You want simplicity.

Do you create clarity now or chaos later?

These decisions are quiet. Their consequences are not.

Common Athlete Mistakes and Financial Parallels

Athletes avoid uncomfortable preparation.

Financially, that leads to confusion and conflict.

Athletes assume someone else will handle it.

Financially, that leads to delays and court involvement.

Athletes wait too long.

Financially, that increases cost and stress.

The scoreboard always reflects preparation.

Winning the Long Game

Estate planning is not about predicting the future.

It is about removing uncertainty.

Clear instructions.

Right decision-makers.

Right timing.

That is how professionals protect what they build.

Athletes who approach estate planning the same way they approach game preparation create peace of mind for themselves and their families. They eliminate unnecessary risk. They take control.

That is winning without needing to be on the field.

Athlete Takeaways

- Estate planning is about control, not age
- Wills and trusts create clarity before pressure hits
- Beneficiary designations matter more than most people realize
- Powers of attorney keep the system functioning if you cannot
- Preparation protects the people you care about most

Chapter 24: Talking About Money With Family

In lacrosse, communication is not optional.

Slides do not work without talking. Clears break down without calls. Offenses stall when players assume instead of communicate. The best teams are loud, clear, and proactive. They talk early, not after a goal is given up.

Money works the same way in families.

Most financial stress inside families is not caused by lack of money. It is caused by lack of conversation. Assumptions replace clarity. Silence replaces planning. By the time the topic finally comes up, emotions are already high and options are limited.

This chapter is about learning how to talk about money with family before pressure forces the conversation.

Opening Story From the Sport

Every lacrosse player has been part of a defensive breakdown that came down to one thing.

Silence.

No call on the slide.

No communication on the crease.

Everyone thought someone else had it covered.

After the goal, fingers point. Frustration builds. But the real issue is simple.

No one talked early enough.

Family money conversations fail for the same reason.

People assume expectations are shared.

They assume intentions are obvious.

They assume "we'll figure it out later."

Later is when things break.

Why Money Conversations Feel So Hard

Money carries emotion.

Pride.

Fear.

Guilt.

Control.

Expectation.

In families, money is rarely just math. It is tied to identity, sacrifice, love, and obligation. Athletes often avoid these conversations because they feel uncomfortable or disrespectful.

But silence does not protect relationships. It strains them.

In lacrosse terms, avoiding communication because you do not want to sound bossy still leads to goals against you. Silence is a decision, even if it does not feel like one.

Talking about money is not about control. It is about clarity.

Teaching Kids About Money

Athletes understand this intuitively.

You do not wait until game day to teach fundamentals.

Kids learn money habits long before they understand money concepts. They learn by watching, not by lectures. Spending habits, saving habits, and stress responses are absorbed quietly.

Teaching kids about money does not require complexity.

It requires consistency.

Simple lessons matter:

- Money is earned, not automatic
- Choices have tradeoffs
- Saving is normal, not punishment
- Spending should be intentional

In lacrosse terms, this is teaching stick skills early. You start with ground balls and passing, not advanced sets. Repetition builds comfort.

Avoid using money as a source of fear or secrecy. Transparency at an age-appropriate level builds confidence instead of anxiety.

College and Young Adults

This stage is where many families struggle the most.

Young adults gain independence while still relying on support. Parents want to help but fear enabling. Athletes transitioning out of structured environments often struggle with budgeting, credit, and long-term thinking.

The mistake families make is avoiding boundaries because they feel uncomfortable.

Support without structure creates confusion.

Structure without communication creates resentment.

In lacrosse terms, this is sending a player on the field without explaining the role. They might work hard and still hurt the team.

Clear conversations matter:

- What support exists?
- For how long?
- Under what conditions?
- What responsibilities are expected?

Financial help should come with education, not silence. The goal is independence, not dependency.

Aging Parents and Caregiving

This is one of the most emotionally charged financial conversations families face.

Parents age.

Health changes.

Costs increase.

Roles reverse.

Many families avoid these conversations because they feel disrespectful or premature. Waiting does not make them easier. It makes them more urgent and less flexible.

Topics that matter:

- Who manages finances if needed?
- What resources exist?
- What expectations are realistic?
- What support is possible without harm?

In lacrosse terms, this is planning substitutions before someone is injured. You do not wait for chaos to assign roles.

Caregiving decisions affect careers, savings, marriages, and mental health. Honest conversations protect everyone involved.

Family Expectations and Boundaries

This is where clarity becomes essential.

Families often operate on unspoken expectations:

- "You'll help if needed."
- "Family takes care of family."
- "Money shouldn't matter."

Those statements feel supportive. Without boundaries, they become pressure.

Boundaries are not selfish.

They are necessary.

In lacrosse terms, boundaries are assignments.

If everyone slides whenever they feel like it, the defense collapses. If roles are clear, the system holds.

Financial boundaries clarify:

- What you can help with
- What you cannot
- What conditions exist
- What tradeoffs are involved

Saying yes without clarity often leads to resentment. Saying no without communication leads to conflict. Boundaries create space for respect.

Why Athletes Struggle With Family Money Conversations

Athletes are conditioned to push through discomfort.

You do not complain.

You do not show weakness.

You handle things quietly.

That mindset works on the field. In family financial conversations, it backfires.

Avoidance is not strength.

Silence is not leadership.

Athletes who learn to communicate calmly and clearly protect relationships and financial stability at the same time.

Coach's Perspective: What Would Your Coach Say?

Your coach would be direct.

"Talk early."

"Call it out."

"Don't assume."

"Protect the team."

"Silence costs us."

They would not accept missed communication as an excuse. Money conversations deserve the same urgency as defensive calls.

Game Situations and Decision Points

Your kids start asking questions about money.

Do you avoid it or teach intentionally?

A young adult needs help.

Do you clarify expectations or hope it works out?

Parents need support.

Do you plan together or wait until crisis hits?

Each choice either builds structure or invites chaos.

Common Athlete Mistakes and Financial Parallels

Athletes avoid uncomfortable conversations.

Financially, that leads to conflict later.

Athletes assume others know their role.

Financially, that leads to misaligned expectations.

Athletes stay silent under pressure.

Financially, that leads to resentment and stress.

Communication is a skill. Like any skill, it improves with reps.

Winning the Long Game

Families that talk about money early make better decisions later.

They argue less.

They plan better.

They protect relationships.

These conversations do not have to be perfect. They have to be honest. Clear communication allows families to adjust, adapt, and support each other without burning out or breaking trust.

In lacrosse, teams that communicate win possession battles.

In life, families that communicate win stability, flexibility, and peace of mind.

Athlete Takeaways

- Silence creates breakdowns. Communication prevents them
- Teaching money early builds confidence, not fear
- Support works best when expectations are clear
- Boundaries protect relationships, not weaken them
- Talk early, talk clearly, and protect the team

Part VI: Winning the Long Game

Every lacrosse season teaches the same truth.

The teams that win at the end are rarely the ones who looked best in the first week. Championships are not decided by one hot stretch, one highlight, or one dominant quarter. They are decided by discipline over time. By teams that value possession, recover from mistakes, communicate under pressure, and stay committed to their system long after the excitement fades.

Money works the same way.

The long game is where financial outcomes are decided. Not in one big investment. Not in one promotion. Not in one purchase. But in thousands of small decisions stacked over years, often when no one is watching and nothing feels urgent.

This final section is about perspective. It ties everything together and brings the focus back to what actually creates lasting success.

Why the Long Game Is Harder Than It Looks

Athletes are wired for competition.

You are trained to focus on the next rep, the next drill, the next opponent. Short-term feedback is constant. You know immediately whether something worked. Money does not give feedback that way.

Financial decisions often feel quiet and unrewarding in the moment. Saving does not feel like winning. Saying no does not feel productive. Patience rarely feels powerful.

In lacrosse terms, this is riding the ball instead of forcing a shot. It does not excite the crowd, but it wins games. The discipline to slow the game down is what separates good teams from great ones.

The long game requires trust in fundamentals when the payoff is delayed.

Consistency Beats Talent Over Time

Every coach knows this.

Talent gets attention.

Consistency gets results.

The most gifted players do not always have the longest careers. The players who show up every day, manage their bodies, learn the system, and adjust as the game changes tend to last.

Financial success follows the same pattern.

You do not need perfect timing.

You do not need insider knowledge.

You do not need to be aggressive.

You need consistency.

Consistent saving.

Consistent investing.

Consistent communication.

Consistent discipline during boring stretches.

Small advantages compound. Small mistakes do too. Over a long horizon, discipline almost always beats intensity.

Adjusting Without Abandoning the System

Great lacrosse teams adjust constantly.

They change matchups.

They tweak schemes.

They manage minutes.

What they do not do is abandon their identity every time something goes wrong.

Financially, the same rule applies.

Life changes.

Careers shift.

Markets move.

Families evolve.

Your plan should adapt, but your principles should not. Chasing trends, panicking during downturns, or constantly reinventing your strategy creates more damage than patience ever will.

The long game rewards players who can adjust while staying anchored.

The Role of Identity After Competition

One of the hardest parts of the long game for former athletes is identity.

Sports provided structure.

Clear roles.

Immediate feedback.

Shared purpose.

When that disappears, many athletes search for the same feeling through money. Bigger purchases. Higher income. More visible success. Those things rarely deliver the fulfillment they promise.

Winning the long game financially is not about replacing competition. It is about redefining it.

The new competition becomes:

- Staying disciplined when others drift
- Making decisions aligned with your values
- Building flexibility instead of pressure
- Creating options instead of obligations

That is a different kind of edge.

What This Section Represents

This final section is not about adding new tactics.

It is about reinforcing mindset.

It reminds you that:

- Financial success is built, not discovered
- The absence of urgency does not mean the absence of importance
- Quiet discipline outperforms loud confidence
- The habits you maintain privately shape the outcomes you see publicly

Just like in lacrosse, the fundamentals never stop mattering. Ground balls still win games in the fourth quarter. Communication still matters when legs are tired. Possession still determines outcomes.

Finishing Strong

The long game does not end.

That is the point.

Money is not something you solve once. It is something you manage through seasons, transitions, and changing roles. The athletes who succeed financially are not the ones who avoid mistakes entirely. They are the ones who recover quickly, stay disciplined, and keep moving forward.

Winning the long game means staying in control.

Staying flexible.

Staying aligned.

Staying patient.

You do not need to be perfect.

You need to stay in the game.

That is how championships are won.

That is how financial independence is built.

That is how life after lacrosse becomes something you lead, not something that happens to you.

Chapter 25: Advisors, Scams, and Long-Term Success

Every lacrosse player eventually learns a hard truth.

You cannot see the whole field by yourself.

On the sideline, coaches see spacing, matchups, fatigue, and tendencies that players in the middle of the action cannot. Teammates communicate slides and rotations you might miss. Trainers catch small issues before they become season-ending injuries. The best players are not the ones who refuse help. They are the ones who know when to ask for it.

Money works the same way.

Long-term financial success is not about doing everything alone. It is about building the right support system, avoiding traps that prey on ego and urgency, and staying disciplined through an entire career and life cycle.

This chapter is about knowing who belongs on your sideline, who should never be near your locker room, and how to keep possession over decades instead of moments.

When to Seek Professional Help

You do not wait until you are down four goals to start coaching.

In lacrosse, help becomes necessary when the game speeds up. When the opponent adjusts. When injuries pile up. When complexity increases. Money reaches that point too.

Professional help makes sense when decisions affect:

- Taxes
- Investments
- Insurance
- Business structures
- Family and estate planning
- Major life transitions

Needing help is not weakness. It is awareness.

In lacrosse terms, this is recognizing when the game has moved beyond individual dodges and requires coordinated offense and defense. Refusing help at that point usually costs possession.

The right advisor allows you to focus on your strengths while someone else helps manage the system.

Types of Financial Advisors

Not all advisors play the same role.

Some focus almost entirely on investments.

Some focus on planning and coordination.

Some sell specific products.

Some act as quarterbacks, helping connect taxes, insurance, investing, and long-term goals.

Titles are less important than alignment.

In lacrosse terms, this is understanding positions. You do not expect a long-stick defender to run the offense. You do not expect a midfielder to anchor the crease defense. Every role matters, but confusion creates breakdowns.

What matters most is:

- How the advisor is compensated
- What they are responsible for
- Who they are accountable to

The best advisor relationships feel like trust, clarity, and communication, not pressure.

Recognizing Scams and Bad Advice

Scams target emotion, not intelligence.

They rely on urgency.

Exclusivity.

Guarantees.

Fear of missing out.

Pressure to act now.

If someone tells you there is no risk, no downside, or no time to think, that is a red flag.

In lacrosse terms, this is biting hard on the first dodge without help defense. The moment you overcommit, you are exposed.

Legitimate strategies:

- Allow time for questions
- Welcome transparency
- Encourage second opinions
- Do not require secrecy

Bad advice often sounds confident. Good advice sounds calm.

Ten Common Financial Mistakes

Athletes make predictable mistakes, not because they are careless, but because the transition away from structured environments is difficult.

1. **Chasing quick wins**
2. Forcing shots instead of moving the ball.
3. **Ignoring taxes**
4. Forgetting that the scoreboard includes penalties.
5. **Overspending early**
6. Burning energy in the first quarter.
7. **Delaying saving and investing**
8. Giving up possession before the game starts.
9. **Concentrating too much risk**

10. Relying on one matchup to win everything.
11. **Avoiding uncomfortable planning**
12. Refusing to watch film.
13. **Trusting the wrong people**
14. Letting the wrong voice into the huddle.
15. **Letting emotion drive decisions**
16. Playing angry instead of smart.
17. **Failing to set boundaries**
18. Losing discipline off the field.
19. **Doing nothing out of fear**
20. Standing still while the game moves.

These mistakes rarely cause immediate collapse. They quietly erode control.

Ten Rules for Long-Term Success

Long-term success is not complicated. It is disciplined.

1. **Live below your means**
2. Control possession.
3. **Save consistently**
4. Win ground balls.
5. **Invest with patience**
6. Trust the system.
7. **Diversify risk**
8. Do not rely on one play.
9. **Manage taxes intentionally**
10. Know the rules of the game.
11. **Protect yourself with insurance**
12. Slide early and often.
13. **Keep systems simple**
14. Complexity causes turnovers.
15. **Communicate clearly**

16. Silence breaks defenses.
17. **Adjust as life changes**
18. Make smart halftime adjustments.
19. **Stay disciplined for the full season**
20. Championships are not won in March.

These rules are not flashy. They work.

Coach's Perspective

What would your coach say?

Handle your business.

Protect possession.

Do not force shots.

Trust the system.

Control what you can control.

Play for the guy next to you.

Finish strong.

Long-term success rewards athletes who stay composed when others panic and stay disciplined when others chase noise.

Winning the Long Game

The long game is not exciting.

It is repetitive.

It is patient.

It is disciplined.

Just like lacrosse.

Financial independence does not come from one perfect decision. It comes from avoiding catastrophic mistakes, stacking small wins, and staying aligned with people who protect your best interests.

You do not need to win every play.

You need to keep possession.

That is how careers are protected.
That is how families are supported.
That is how life after lacrosse becomes intentional instead of reactive.

Athlete Takeaways

- Protect possession by building the right financial sideline
- If someone rushes you, they do not belong in the huddle
- Small mistakes compound like turnovers
- Discipline and patience win long seasons
- The goal is not a highlight, it is control of the game

Chapter 26: Losing the Schedule and Rebuilding Structure

One of the biggest shocks after lacrosse is not physical.

It is structural.

For most of your playing career, your life ran on a calendar someone else built. Practice times. Lift sessions. Film. Team meetings. Travel. Even rest was scheduled. You did not have to decide when to show up. You just showed up.

Then the season ends.

And the schedule disappears.

No more mandatory practices. No coach checking attendance. No whistle to reset focus. What used to be enforced discipline becomes optional discipline. That transition quietly breaks a lot of former athletes, not because they became lazy, but because the system that created consistency is gone.

From Mandatory Workouts to Optional Discipline

In lacrosse, discipline is baked into the structure.

If practice starts at 3:30, you are there early. If lifts are at 6:00 a.m., you figure it out. Miss reps and it shows up in conditioning, stick skills, and playing time. The structure forces effort whether motivation is high or low.

After sports, that pressure disappears.

No one makes you save money.

No one checks if you reviewed your budget.

No one calls you out for skipping planning.

In lacrosse terms, this is like going from a fully organized practice plan to an open field with a bucket of balls and no coach. Some players still get better. Most drift.

Optional discipline is harder than mandatory discipline because there is no immediate consequence for skipping it. You can miss a week of budgeting. Delay retirement contributions. Ignore insurance decisions. Nothing happens right away.

That delay is dangerous.

How Lack of Structure Quietly Breaks Financial Habits

Most financial breakdowns are not dramatic.

They are quiet.

Saving becomes inconsistent.

Bills get paid late.

Credit card balances creep up.

Long-term goals get pushed aside for short-term comfort.

There is no single bad decision. Just erosion.

In lacrosse, this looks like missed footwork drills, sloppy passes, and poor spacing. You are still playing, but execution drops. Over time, the gap widens between where you are and where you thought you would be.

Athletes are used to accountability. When it disappears, habits often weaken unless new systems replace the old ones.

Money is especially vulnerable because feedback is delayed. You do not feel the consequences of skipping savings today. You feel them years later when options are limited.

Why Former Athletes Struggle With Self-Directed Structure

Lacrosse players thrive in organized environments.

Clear roles. Clear expectations. Clear consequences.

After sports, the rules are fuzzy. Work schedules vary. Income may fluctuate. No one tells you how often to review finances or what good execution looks like. Former athletes often wait for structure that never arrives.

This leads to frustration and drift.

In lacrosse terms, it is like waiting for a coach to call plays in a pickup game. If you do not take ownership, the game stays chaotic.

Replacing Practice Schedules With Personal Systems

Structure does not disappear. It has to be rebuilt.

The athletes who succeed financially after sports replace external structure with internal systems. They do not rely on motivation. They rely on routines.

Financial systems function like practice plans.

Automatic savings replace mandatory lifts.

Scheduled reviews replace film sessions.

Rules replace constant decision-making.

Examples of effective systems include:

- Automatic transfers to savings and investment accounts on payday
- Fixed dates each month for bill payments
- Quarterly or annual financial check-ins on the calendar
- Simple rules like saving raises before upgrading lifestyle

In lacrosse terms, this is self-coached training. You design the drill. You show up. You run it whether you feel like it or not.

The goal is not intensity.

The goal is rhythm.

Discipline Is Easier When Decisions Are Removed

Great teams reduce decision-making under pressure.

You do not debate whether to slide.

You do not guess the clear.

You execute what you practiced.

Financial discipline works the same way. When systems are in place, behavior happens automatically. When systems are missing, emotions take over.

If you have to decide every month whether to save, you will eventually decide not to. If savings happen automatically, discipline becomes default.

Coach's Perspective

A coach would not sugarcoat this.

Nobody is setting your calendar anymore.

Nobody is checking your reps.

Nobody is calling you out when you drift.

That does not mean it does not matter.

A coach would say:

- "Discipline is a choice now."
- "Do not drift."
- "Build your own structure."
- "How you practice is how you play."
- "Nobody cares. Work harder."

The absence of structure is not freedom.

It is risk.

Game Situations and Decision Points

Situation 1: You get paid and there is money left over.

Do you wait to see what happens, or does your system already tell that money where to go?

Situation 2: You miss a month of saving.

Do you quit the plan or reset and get back into rhythm?

Situation 3: No one is watching your financial habits.

Do you still show up and execute?

What you do in these moments determines long-term outcomes.

Common Athlete Mistakes and Financial Parallels

Athletes rely on external accountability.

Financially, that leads to inconsistency.

Athletes underestimate drift.

Financially, that leads to lost years of compounding.

Athletes avoid systems because they feel restrictive.

Financially, that leads to chaos.

Winning the Long Game

Rebuilding structure after sports is one of the most important skills a former athlete can develop.

Systems replace coaches.

Calendars replace practice plans.

Discipline becomes internal.

Those who rebuild structure early protect their future. Those who do not often look back wondering where the time went.

The game did not get easier.

The rules just changed.

Athlete Takeaways

- Losing the schedule is normal. Drifting is optional.
- Optional discipline is harder than mandatory discipline.
- Systems beat motivation every time.
- Build financial routines the same way you built practice habits.
- What you do when no one is watching determines the final score.

Chapter 27: From Teammates to Coworkers

One of the most disorienting transitions after lacrosse has nothing to do with fitness, skill, or work ethic.

It is cultural.

For most of your athletic life, you operated inside a system built on clarity. Roles were defined. Authority was visible. Feedback was direct. Performance was measured every day. You knew exactly where you stood because the structure told you.

Then you enter the workplace.

The structure fades. Expectations blur. Feedback becomes indirect or nonexistent. Authority is less obvious. Success is harder to measure. Many former lacrosse players feel frustrated or stalled not because they lack ability, but because the environment no longer operates the way they were trained to succeed.

This shift affects more than job satisfaction. It affects income growth, confidence, and long-term career stability.

Why the Workplace Feels Foreign After Sports

Lacrosse environments are honest.

If you earn reps in practice, you play more.

If you slack, it shows immediately.

If you perform, your role expands.

The scoreboard, film, and depth chart provide constant feedback.

Workplaces rarely function this way.

Performance metrics are often vague. Expectations are implied instead of stated. Promotions are influenced by timing, perception, and relationships as much as output. This feels unsettling for athletes who are used to objective evaluation.

In lacrosse terms, this is like playing a full game with no scoreboard. You are running, competing, and working hard, but you do not know the score or how the coaches are judging performance.

Without clarity, former athletes often default to one of two mistakes. They either overwork quietly and hope effort gets noticed, or they disengage out of frustration when effort does not translate into results.

Neither leads to growth.

Authority Without Coaches

In lacrosse, authority is obvious.

Head coaches set the tone. Assistants run drills. Captains lead on the field. Accountability is enforced in real time. If something is wrong, you hear about it.

In many workplaces, authority is less clear.

Managers may avoid confrontation. Decision-makers may sit two layers above you. Influence may not match job titles. Understanding who actually sets priorities matters far more than what the organizational chart shows.

Former athletes often struggle here because they wait for direction that never comes.

In lacrosse, waiting for instruction is often correct. In the workplace, waiting can stall progress. Initiative matters more. Asking questions matters more. Clarifying expectations matters more.

In lacrosse terms, this is like standing still waiting for a coach to call a set while the defense adjusts and the shot clock runs down. You have to recognize the moment and move.

Feedback Without Film

Athletes are raised on film.

You see mistakes immediately. You review reps. You correct technique. Feedback is specific and often blunt. Improvement is constant because information is constant.

In the workplace, feedback is often delayed, softened, or avoided entirely.

You may not know you are underperforming until a review months later. You may not know what you are doing well because no one says it. Silence becomes the default.

In lacrosse terms, this is playing an entire season without film sessions. You have to self-scout.

Former athletes who adapt learn to ask for feedback instead of waiting for it. They schedule check-ins. They ask clear questions. They seek clarity on priorities and performance standards.

Those who do not often feel blindsided when outcomes do not match effort.

Politics, Ambiguity, and Unclear Expectations

Workplaces involve politics.

Relationships matter.

Perception matters.

Timing matters.

For athletes, this can feel uncomfortable. Lacrosse teaches you that effort and execution should speak for themselves. In many professional environments, effort alone is not enough if no one understands your contribution or sees your value.

Ignoring politics does not make them disappear.

Navigating politics does not mean compromising values. It means understanding the environment so your work has impact.

In lacrosse terms, this is learning scouting reports. You still play your game, but you adjust based on matchups, tendencies, and context.

Clear communication protects opportunity. Silence rarely does.

How This Impacts Income Growth and Career Stability

Confusion slows progress.

When expectations are unclear, effort gets misdirected. When feedback is missing, improvement stalls. When relationships are ignored, opportunities shrink.

Former athletes who adapt tend to grow faster because they transfer athletic skills into professional ones.

They communicate early.

They seek clarity.

They build relationships.

They advocate for themselves.

Those who do not often feel stuck, underpaid, or overlooked despite working hard.

Income growth is rarely automatic. It is influenced by visibility, timing, and alignment with organizational priorities. Career stability depends on understanding the system you are playing in, not just how hard you grind.

Translating Team Skills Into Workplace Success

The skills that made you successful in lacrosse still matter. They just show up differently.

Discipline becomes reliability.

Preparation becomes competence.

Leadership becomes communication.

Teamwork becomes collaboration.

The biggest adjustment is learning to define success without a depth chart. You have to build your own scoreboard through feedback, results, and relationships.

Coach's Perspective

A coach would be direct.

- "Learn the system."
- "Do not wait for instructions."
- "Ask for feedback."
- "Communicate clearly."
- "Take ownership."

A coach would remind you that responsibility does not disappear when structure changes. It increases.

You are still responsible for your development.

Game Situations and Decision Points

Situation 1: You are unsure what matters most in your role.

Do you guess, or do you ask for clarity?

Situation 2: You want advancement.

Do you wait quietly, or do you communicate goals and progress?

Situation 3: You feel frustrated by politics.

Do you disengage, or do you learn how to navigate the environment professionally?

Awareness changes outcomes.

Common Athlete Mistakes and Financial Parallels

Athletes wait for direction.

Financially and professionally, that stalls income growth.

Athletes avoid politics entirely.

Financially and professionally, that limits opportunity.

Athletes expect fairness instead of clarity.

Financially and professionally, that leads to frustration.

Winning the Long Game

The workplace is not the locker room. The rules are different, but success is still possible.

Former lacrosse players who adapt without losing discipline build stable, growing careers. They stop waiting for whistles. They stop assuming effort speaks for itself. They learn to communicate, self-evaluate, and advocate.

The game did not end.

The system changed.

Those who learn the new system keep moving forward.

Athlete Takeaways

- The workplace has no scoreboard. You must create clarity.
- Authority and feedback are less obvious. Ask instead of waiting.
- Politics and perception matter whether you like them or not.
- Communication protects income growth and opportunity.
- Adaptation, not effort alone, builds long-term career stability.

Chapter 28: When No One Is Watching Anymore

One of the hardest adjustments after lacrosse does not show up on a résumé or a bank statement.

It shows up quietly, over time.

For most of your athletic life, accountability was constant. Coaches watched every rep. Teammates noticed effort. Film did not lie. If you skipped preparation, it showed immediately on the field. Pressure was built into the environment.

Then the season ends.

No more mandatory workouts.

No more practice schedule.

No one tracking effort.

No scoreboard reminding you what matters.

When no one is watching anymore, discipline becomes optional. That transition creates a gap many former athletes do not see coming.

The Discipline Gap After Accountability Disappears

Lacrosse is built on accountability.

Miss a slide and your teammate pays for it.

Skip a clear and possession flips.

Take a play off and the goal horn sounds.

Consequences are immediate.

After sports, consequences are delayed.

You can skip saving.

You can overspend.

You can delay planning.

Nothing happens right away.

That delay is dangerous.

In lacrosse terms, this is like playing pickup with no score kept. The intensity drops unless you bring it yourself. The fundamentals slip. Bad habits creep in because nothing forces correction.

Former athletes are not undisciplined. They are unprotected from drift.

Why Former Athletes Self-Sabotage Without Pressure

Pressure sharpens focus.

Deadlines, depth charts, and competition create urgency. When those disappear, comfort often replaces discipline. Netflix replaces training. Spending replaces saving. Short-term relief replaces long-term progress.

This is rarely intentional.

Self-sabotage does not look like blowing everything up. It looks like small compromises repeated over time.

In lacrosse terms, it is jogging through a drill because no coach is watching. One rep does not matter. Then another. Then it becomes normal.

Money works the same way.

Small decisions compound quietly. Skipping one contribution. Carrying one balance. Ignoring one account. Years later, the damage shows up all at once.

Comfort vs Growth Decisions

Every decision lives on a spectrum between comfort and growth.

Comfort feels good now.

Growth feels uncomfortable now but pays off later.

In lacrosse, comfort is settling for a low-angle shot early in the possession.

Growth is moving the ball, trusting teammates, and waiting for a better look.

Financially, comfort looks like lifestyle inflation. Convenience spending. Avoiding planning because it feels overwhelming. Growth looks like saving when it is not exciting, investing when it feels boring, and sticking to systems when motivation fades.

Former athletes are used to discomfort in training. The challenge is learning to choose discomfort when there is no coach demanding it.

Translating "Grind Culture" Into Adult Life

Grind culture does not translate cleanly.

In sports, grinding harder often works because structure supports recovery and direction. In adult life, grinding without systems leads to burnout.

Working more hours does not automatically improve finances. Hustling without a plan creates chaos. Constant intensity without recovery erodes consistency.

In lacrosse terms, this is sprinting every shift without understanding spacing or timing. You look busy, but the offense stalls.

Financial progress comes from rhythm, not constant strain. Automatic systems. Scheduled reviews. Clear rules. Sustainable habits.

The goal is not to outwork everyone forever. The goal is to build a structure that works even when motivation drops.

Why Money Mistakes Show Up Years Later

Money provides delayed feedback.

Overspending today creates stress years later.

Skipping investing now limits options decades later.

Poor decisions compound quietly.

In lacrosse, you can blow an assignment early in the game and not feel it until the fourth quarter. The score tightens. Fatigue sets in. Suddenly, the margin is gone.

Financial mistakes work the same way. The pain shows up long after the decision.

That is why former athletes often feel confused when life feels harder later. The habits were slipping quietly when no one was watching.

Building Discipline Without an Audience

Discipline after sports has to be internal.

No one is going to blow the whistle.

No one is going to bench you.

No one is going to force structure.

You have to build it.

Automatic transfers replace mandatory workouts.

Calendars replace practice schedules.

Rules replace motivation.

In lacrosse terms, this is self-coached training. You show up because you decided it matters, not because someone is checking attendance.

Discipline without an audience is harder, but it is more powerful.

Coach's Perspective

A coach would be blunt.

- "Nobody is watching now."
- "That does not mean it does not matter."
- "Comfort is the enemy."
- "Discipline is your responsibility."
- "Choose growth."

A coach would remind you that effort without structure fades. Systems protect effort when motivation disappears.

Game Situations and Decision Points

Situation 1: You are tired and no one will know if you skip a habit.

Do you choose comfort or consistency?

Situation 2: The payoff feels far away.

Do you trust the process or chase relief?

Situation 3: Life feels unstructured.

Do you build systems or drift?

What you do when no one is watching defines outcomes.

Common Athlete Mistakes and Financial Parallels

Athletes rely on external pressure.

Financially, that leads to drift.

Athletes chase comfort after competition ends.

Financially, that leads to overspending and missed opportunities.

Athletes confuse grind with progress.

Financially, that leads to burnout instead of consistency.

Winning the Long Game

The most important habits are the ones you maintain privately.

When no one is watching.

When motivation is low.

When progress feels invisible.

Former lacrosse players who succeed financially are not louder or flashier. They are consistent. They rebuild structure early. They replace accountability with systems.

The uniform comes off.

The discipline must stay.

Athlete Takeaways

- When the whistles stop, discipline becomes your responsibility
- Comfort choices feel good now but cost you later
- Grind without structure leads to burnout, not progress
- Systems replace motivation when no one is watching
- What you do in private shows up on the scoreboard years later

Chapter 29: Redefining Winning After the Uniform Comes Off

For most of your life in lacrosse, winning was obvious.

Goals on the board.

Minutes on the field.

Depth charts.

Conference titles.

Championship weekends.

You never had to guess if you were improving. The scoreboard told you. Film confirmed it. Coaches reinforced it. Teammates held you accountable.

Then the uniform comes off.

The scoreboard disappears, but the competitive instinct does not. That instinct still wants to win. Still wants progress. Still wants validation. Without clear metrics, many former athletes replace performance with status without realizing it.

What used to be about mastery quietly becomes about comparison.

Why Chasing Status Replaces Chasing Performance

Lacrosse rewards performance.

If you see the field well, you play.

If you protect possession, you stay on.

If you produce, you earn trust.

Life rewards appearance more than we like to admit.

Income. Job titles. Houses. Cars. Social media highlights. These become proxies for success when real performance metrics disappear.

In lacrosse terms, this is playing for the crowd instead of running the offense. The play looks impressive, but it does not always lead to wins.

Status provides fast validation. Performance provides lasting fulfillment.

When former athletes feel unsettled, status becomes tempting because it is visible and measurable. You can point to it. Post it. Compare it. That does not mean it reflects progress.

Income vs Fulfillment

Income matters. It creates stability. It creates options. It reduces stress.

But income alone is not fulfillment.

Many former athletes reach income milestones and still feel empty. The clarity of competition is gone. The identity feels blurred. The days feel disconnected from purpose.

In lacrosse terms, this is putting up points on a losing team. The stats look fine. The feeling does not.

Fulfillment comes from alignment. Growth. Contribution. Control over time. Using your skills in ways that matter to you.

Income supports fulfillment. It does not replace it.

When income becomes the only scoreboard, decisions start drifting. You chase more without asking why. You accept tradeoffs that quietly erode satisfaction.

Titles, Houses, Cars, and Comparison Traps

Comparison is constant.

Former teammates become measuring sticks.

Social media turns highlights into daily pressure.

Lifestyle inflation masquerades as progress.

There is always someone ahead. Someone earning more. Someone posting better angles. Someone appearing to win harder.

In lacrosse terms, this is chasing highlight goals instead of winning possessions. You start forcing shots that were never there.

Comparison distorts decision-making. It pushes spending higher. Risk tolerance beyond comfort. Career moves that look good but feel wrong.

Status symbols are loud. Fulfillment is quiet.

What Success Actually Looks Like in Your 30s and 40s

Success evolves.

In your 30s and 40s, winning looks different than it did at 20.

It looks like flexibility.

It looks like health.

It looks like control over your schedule.

It looks like financial stability without anxiety.

It looks like presence with people who matter.

These wins do not show up on a stat sheet. They show up in how you feel on Monday mornings. In how you sleep. In how decisions feel instead of how they look.

Former athletes who redefine success early make better decisions. They stop chasing every opportunity and start choosing intentionally.

Those who do not often feel stuck chasing a version of winning that no longer fits.

Building a New Scoreboard

You cannot win a game if you do not know the score.

After sports, you need new metrics.

Peace of mind.

Progress toward long-term goals.

Alignment with values.

Consistency over time.

Optionality instead of pressure.

In lacrosse terms, this is redefining the game plan. Same fundamentals.

Different objective.

A new scoreboard does not mean lowering standards. It means raising them. You measure what actually matters instead of what gets applause.

The Cost of Not Redefining Winning

When winning stays undefined, drift sets in.

Spending creeps up.

Career decisions feel reactive.

Comparison drives choices.

Fulfillment gets postponed.

Former athletes are especially vulnerable because they are wired to compete. Without a clear target, competition turns inward or outward in unhealthy ways.

Redefining winning protects your finances and your identity.

Coach's Perspective

A coach would not sugarcoat this.

- "Define the game you are playing."
- "Stop chasing the crowd."
- "Execution beats flash."
- "Control what you can control."
- "Win on your terms."

A coach would remind you that championships are not won by noise. They are won by alignment, discipline, and clarity.

Game Situations and Decision Points

Situation 1: You see a former teammate's success online.

Do you compare or refocus?

Situation 2: You hit an income milestone.

Do you ask what is next or what matters?

Situation 3: You feel pressure to upgrade your lifestyle.

Do you chase status or protect flexibility?

The scoreboard you choose determines the plays you call.

Common Athlete Mistakes and Financial Parallels

Athletes chase validation.

Financially, that leads to overspending.

Athletes avoid introspection.

Financially, that leads to misaligned goals.

Athletes confuse winning with visibility.

Financially, that leads to regret.

Winning the Long Game

Redefining winning is not quitting competition.

It is choosing a better one.

When success aligns with who you are and how you want to live, discipline becomes easier. Decisions feel cleaner. Progress feels real again.

The uniform comes off.

The competitive instinct stays.

The definition of winning must evolve.

Athlete Takeaways

- Status is loud, fulfillment is earned quietly
- Income supports winning but does not define it
- Comparison distorts shot selection and decision-making
- Success in your 30s and 40s is about flexibility and control
- Build a new scoreboard or end up chasing the wrong game

Chapter 30: Staying Connected Without Living in the Past

One of the quiet losses after lacrosse is not competition.

It is connection.

The locker room disappears.

Daily contact fades.

Shared struggle is replaced by individual schedules.

Most athletes do not realize how much of their identity was shaped by being part of a team until that team is gone. Practices end. Group travel stops. The constant presence of people who understand your grind vanishes almost overnight.

What remains is silence.

Staying connected matters.

Living in the past does not.

The difference between the two determines whether former athletes grow or stall after the uniform comes off.

The Role of Community, Mentorship, and New Locker Rooms

Lacrosse is a team sport built on trust.

You rely on slides.

You communicate constantly.

You know where help is coming from.

Performance improves when accountability and support are shared.

After sports, that structure disappears unless it is rebuilt intentionally.

New locker rooms exist. They just look different.

Work teams.

Professional groups.

Alumni networks.

Volunteer organizations.

Faith communities.

Peer groups of former athletes.

These environments recreate the core elements athletes need: shared standards, accountability, and belonging.

Mentorship matters even more.

In lacrosse, younger players develop faster when older players model habits, preparation, and composure. Life works the same way. Learning from people a few steps ahead shortens the learning curve and reduces unnecessary mistakes.

Isolation slows growth. Community accelerates it.

Why Isolation Hits Former Athletes Hard

Isolation is dangerous because it is subtle.

There is no injury report.

No coach calling it out.

No obvious failure point.

Former athletes go from constant interaction to independent routines. Busy schedules mask loneliness. Productivity disguises disconnection.

Without teammates, feedback disappears. Motivation fades. Perspective narrows.

In lacrosse terms, this is playing defense without communication. Everyone thinks they are doing their job, but breakdowns happen quietly and repeatedly.

Isolation often shows up as:

- Overworking to replace purpose

- Withdrawing socially
- Avoiding reflection
- Losing motivation without knowing why

Former athletes are wired for shared effort. When that disappears, performance in life and finances suffers.

Finding Purpose Without the Team

Purpose does not disappear when the team does.

It changes.

Many former athletes struggle because they chase the exact feeling sports gave them instead of building something new. They want the adrenaline, the crowd, the identity, the clear role.

That version of purpose does not return.

In lacrosse terms, this is refusing to adapt your role when the lineup changes. You cannot play the same position forever.

Purpose after sports often comes from:

- Leadership
- Teaching
- Mentoring
- Building something meaningful
- Contributing to others

These forms of purpose are quieter than competition but more sustainable.

Impact replaces applause.

Former athletes who redefine purpose stop chasing the past and start building forward.

Healthy Nostalgia vs Being Stuck

Remembering your playing days is normal.

Celebrating big wins.

Laughing about road trips.

Sharing stories with teammates.

That is healthy nostalgia.

Being stuck shows up when identity stops evolving.

If every story ends with what you used to do, growth has stalled.

If every comparison points backward, progress is blocked.

If your best moments are always behind you, the present feels empty.

In lacrosse terms, this is watching old game film instead of preparing for the next opponent.

The past should inform you, not define you.

Creating a Forward-Looking Identity

Identity has to move forward.

You are not an athlete who used to play lacrosse.

You are a person who learned discipline, resilience, teamwork, and accountability through lacrosse.

Those traits still matter.

In lacrosse terms, this is transferring skills to a new system. The plays change. The fundamentals remain.

A forward-looking identity focuses on:

- Who you are becoming
- What you are building
- How your skills translate now
- Where you want to grow next

When identity evolves, decisions improve. Finances stabilize. Confidence returns.

How Disconnection Affects Financial Decisions

Isolation does not just affect emotions. It affects money.

Without accountability, spending drifts.

Without perspective, risk tolerance skews.

Without guidance, mistakes compound.

Former athletes often make poor financial decisions not because they lack discipline, but because they lack community.

In lacrosse terms, this is forcing clears alone instead of trusting outlets. Possession gets lost.

Connection provides feedback. Feedback protects decisions.

Coach's Perspective

A coach would challenge you directly.

- "Honor what you built."
- "Do not live there."
- "Find your next team."
- "Stay connected."
- "Keep growing."

A coach would remind you that stagnation is the real loss, not the end of competition.

Game Situations and Decision Points

Situation 1: You feel disconnected after leaving sports.

Do you isolate or seek community?

Situation 2: You miss the locker room.

Do you rebuild structure or relive memories?

Situation 3: Your identity feels unclear.

Do you evolve or stay attached to the past?

Every choice either builds forward momentum or keeps you anchored.

Common Athlete Mistakes and Financial Parallels

Athletes cling to past identity.

Financially, that leads to stagnation.

Athletes isolate.

Financially, that leads to poor decisions.

Athletes resist change.

Financially, that limits opportunity.

Winning the Long Game

Staying connected does not mean staying the same.

Growth requires new relationships, new roles, and new challenges. Former lacrosse players who thrive are not the ones who forget the past. They are the ones who use it as fuel instead of an anchor.

The game continues.

The setting changes.

The skills still apply.

Athlete Takeaways

- Community fuels growth long after competition ends
- Isolation quietly erodes motivation and clarity
- Purpose evolves beyond the team and the scoreboard
- Honor the past without letting it trap you
- Build a forward-looking identity and keep moving forward

Disclaimers

Educational Purpose Only

This book is for **educational purposes only**.

The information provided in **Lacrosse Money 101** is intended to help readers understand general financial concepts using **lacrosse-based analogies**. It is **not** individualized financial, investment, tax, legal, or insurance advice.

Every financial situation is different. Your goals, income, family circumstances, risk tolerance, and time horizon are unique. What works for one athlete, family, or professional may not be appropriate for another.

Not Financial, Investment, or Legal Advice

Nothing in this book should be interpreted as a recommendation to buy, sell, or hold any specific investment, financial product, insurance policy, or strategy.

This book does **not** replace advice from qualified professionals, including but not limited to:

- Financial advisors
- Accountants or tax professionals
- Attorneys
- Insurance professionals

Before making financial decisions, readers should consult professionals who can evaluate their individual situation and provide guidance tailored to their needs.

No Guarantees or Promises of Results

All investing involves risk, including the possible loss of principal.

Past performance does not guarantee future results. Markets fluctuate. Economic conditions change. Outcomes cannot be predicted or guaranteed.

The examples, scenarios, and illustrations used in this book are for **educational purposes only**. They may not reflect actual results, real-world performance, or outcomes experienced by any individual.

Tax and Legal Information

Any discussion of taxes, retirement accounts, estate planning, or legal structures is **general in nature** and intended solely for educational context.

Tax laws and regulations change frequently and vary by jurisdiction. Legal requirements differ based on location, governing bodies, and personal circumstances.

Readers should seek personalized tax or legal advice from qualified professionals before acting on any information related to these topics.

Athlete and Career Considerations

This book discusses financial topics as they relate to athletes and former athletes, including career transitions, income variability, and life after competition.

It does **not** provide career placement services, employment advice, contract negotiation services, or guarantees related to income, compensation, endorsements, or career success.

Use of Analogies

Lacrosse and sports analogies are used throughout this book to make financial concepts easier to understand.

These analogies are **educational tools only** and should not be interpreted literally. Financial decisions require analysis beyond analogy, including personal context, risk assessment, and professional guidance.

Personal Responsibility

By reading this book, you acknowledge and agree that:

- You are responsible for your own financial decisions
- You understand that financial outcomes involve uncertainty and risk
- You agree to seek appropriate professional guidance when needed

Education can improve decision-making, but responsibility always remains with the individual.

Contact Information

If you would like to learn more about the concepts discussed in this book or explore additional educational resources, **Pat Brown** can be found through public platforms including LinkedIn, Twitter, and via Google search.

For questions specifically related to **Lacrosse Money 101**, you may contact:

info@lacrossemoney101.com

Final Reminder

Financial success is built over time through **discipline, planning, and consistency**.

This book provides a **framework**, not a guarantee.

Use it as a guide, not as a substitute for professional advice.

Glossary of Lacrosse and Financial Terms

This glossary connects key financial concepts to familiar ideas from **lacrosse**, making money easier to understand through the language, structure, and discipline players already know.

Asset Allocation

Financial Definition:

How money is divided among different investment types such as stocks, bonds, and cash to balance risk and return.

Lacrosse Comparison:

How minutes, matchups, and responsibilities are distributed across the field. Too much focus on one player or one strategy without balance creates breakdowns.

Assets

Financial Definition:

Things you own that have value, such as cash, investments, real estate, or retirement accounts.

Lacrosse Comparison:

Your strengths as a player. Stick skills, speed, conditioning, IQ, and experience that contribute to winning possessions.

Bonds

Financial Definition:

Loans made to governments or companies that pay interest and return principal over time.

Lacrosse Comparison:

Solid team defense. Not flashy, but essential for stability when the game tightens.

Budget

Financial Definition:

A plan for how income is allocated toward expenses, savings, and goals.

Lacrosse Comparison:

The offensive set. Without structure and timing, possessions end in turnovers.

Cash Flow

Financial Definition:

Money coming in versus money going out.

Lacrosse Comparison:

Substitution and stamina management. Burn too much energy early, and you fade late.

Compounding

Financial Definition:

Earnings that generate additional earnings over time.

Lacrosse Comparison:

Daily reps. Each practice builds on the last and makes execution easier under pressure.

Credit

Financial Definition:

The ability to borrow money with the promise of repayment.

Lacrosse Comparison:

Trust from coaches and teammates. Earned slowly, lost quickly, and powerful when respected.

Debt

Financial Definition:

Money borrowed that must be repaid, often with interest.

Lacrosse Comparison:

Playing out of position for too long. Manageable briefly, damaging if prolonged.

Diversification

Financial Definition:

Spreading investments across different assets to reduce risk.

Lacrosse Comparison:

Balanced scoring. You cannot rely on one dodger or one shooter every possession.

Emergency Fund

Financial Definition:

Savings set aside for unexpected expenses.

Lacrosse Comparison:

The slide package. You hope you do not need it, but it saves goals when things break down.

ETF (Exchange-Traded Fund)

Financial Definition:

A fund that holds many investments and trades like a stock.

Lacrosse Comparison:

Team offense. Shared effort instead of hero ball.

Fees / Expense Ratios

Financial Definition:

Costs associated with managing investments.

Lacrosse Comparison:

Poor spacing and sloppy clears. Small mistakes that quietly cost possessions.

Growth Investing

Financial Definition:

Investing in companies expected to grow faster than average.

Lacrosse Comparison:

Aggressive offense. Higher upside, but it requires discipline and fundamentals.

Insurance

Financial Definition:

Protection against financial loss from unexpected events.

Lacrosse Comparison:

Protective gear. You do not step on the field without it when contact increases.

Liquidity

Financial Definition:

How easily money can be accessed without penalty or delay.

Lacrosse Comparison:

Transition speed. The ability to adjust quickly when the game changes.

Net Worth

Financial Definition:

Assets minus liabilities.

Lacrosse Comparison:

The scoreboard at the end of the game. Not one play, the full result.

Rebalancing

Financial Definition:

Adjusting investments back to their intended mix over time.

Lacrosse Comparison:

Mid-game adjustments to restore spacing and matchups.

Risk

Financial Definition:

The chance that outcomes differ from expectations, including loss.

Lacrosse Comparison:

Dodging into traffic. Higher reward comes with higher exposure.

Roth IRA

Financial Definition:

A retirement account where money grows tax-free if rules are followed.

Lacrosse Comparison:

Extra conditioning early so the fourth quarter feels easier.

Stocks

Financial Definition:

Ownership shares in a company.

Lacrosse Comparison:

Primary attackers. They drive scoring but need support to succeed.

Tax-Advantaged Accounts

Financial Definition:

Accounts that provide tax benefits, often with rules and restrictions.

Lacrosse Comparison:

Structured practice plans. Rules exist to produce better outcomes.

Volatility

Financial Definition:

Short-term ups and downs in market value.

Lacrosse Comparison:

Loose-ball chaos. Normal movement unless you panic.

Permanent Loss

Financial Definition:

Money that cannot recover due to poor decisions or panic.

Lacrosse Comparison:

An unforced turnover that leads directly to a goal.

Total Return

Financial Definition:

Investment return from both price growth and income.

Lacrosse Comparison:

The full stat line. Goals, assists, and ground balls all count.

Value Investing

Financial Definition:

Investing in assets believed to be undervalued.

Lacrosse Comparison:

Smart shot selection. Less flash, more efficiency.

Yield

Financial Definition:

Income generated from an investment.

Lacrosse Comparison:

Consistent scoring. Not spectacular, but dependable.

Final Note

This glossary reinforces one core principle:

Financial success, like success in **lacrosse**, comes from balance, discipline, timing, and repetition.

That philosophy runs through **Lacrosse Money 101** and well beyond the final whistle.

Pat Brown OLB, University of Kansas

Made in the USA
Monee, IL
04 November 2026

67386747R00144